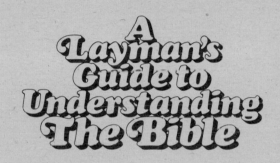

A
Layman's
Guide to
Understanding
The Bible

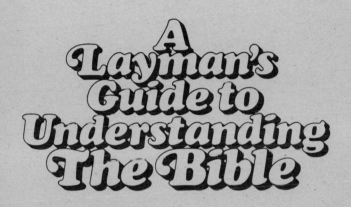

A Layman's Guide to Understanding The Bible

W. W. Orr

Harvest House Publishers
Irvine, California 92714

A LAYMAN'S GUIDE TO UNDERSTANDING THE BIBLE

Copyright © 1978 Harvest House Publishers
Irvine, California 92714
Library of Congress Catalog Card Number: 77-93517
ISBN # 0-89081-118-0

Printed in the United States of America

Preface

● **The Bible** is the most priceless possession of the human race. Why? Because it is the Book come from God, containing God's unique and complete revelation to man. In the very nature of the case the Bible must needs be inerrent, infallible and eternal. And it is! Such claims are satisfactorily proved by many evidences. Over the centuries a multitude of men and women have placed their entire confidence in the truthfulness of the Bible. Some have died rather than renounce its veracity. More have lived godly, unselfish lives by means of its precepts. It stands above every other book. It welcomes investigation. It challenges any test. It is impervious to destruction. It is applicable to every race. It is perennial in its appeal. It is the Book of books from the King of kings.

● **The Old Testament** is a library of 39 inspired books. They are divinely given to be a source of wisdom and instruction. Together they form a mosaic of God's revelation to the particular age of which they are a part. The Old Testament is largely the work of over 30 men, inspired of God. Approximately eleven hundred years were spent in its composition. It is mostly the story of the fortunes of a rather small, semi-obscure race of people called the Jews. God, however, has chosen this race as a means of revealing His will and character, and as a vehicle to convey spiritual truth to the world. The Old Testament is in itself incomplete. Being progressive in character and prophetic in vision, it anticipates and demands the complementary accomplishments, unfolding and explaining of truth in the New Testament.

● **The New Testament** is made up of 27 books each having

its theme, purpose, development and occasion of writing. All are unique and form their own complete and perfect message to the entire family of humanity for all time but as a whole is utterly dependent upon the Old. Linked together by hundreds of direct quotations, indirect references, and fulfillments of types and figures, it is the second and final half of the whole of God's revealed truth. Conversely, the Old is dependent upon the New. All the problems, unexplained difficulties, and unanswered questions which the Old Testament leaves high in the air, are brought safely down and completely solved before the final book, Revelation, closes.

• **Each Book** has its own particular character. In the sacred canon of God's appointment, each book has its separate ministry. For instance, the book of Job explains the mystery of human suffering. The book of Proverbs furnishes pegs upon which to hang the short, easy-to-remember gems of wisdom for life. The book of Psalms offers lyrics to sing for every conceivable mood of the heart. It is of value to know the inner nature of the individual book before you attempt to study it. You should know who wrote it, why he wrote it, the people to whom it was written, the main divisions, and the chief characters.
• **There Is No Substitute** for the simple reading of the Scriptures. It is not sufficient to know "about" the book or its contents. These facts may be helpful and enlightening. But the book must be read and reread. It is always best to read the particular book at a sitting, if possible. In this way the reader can catch the entire message. But if this is not always convenient, the reader should remember that the chapter divisions are "man-made" and could possibly be in the wrong place, and sometimes do disparagement to the complete thought of the writer.
• **God Is Interested** in the use of His Book. To this end, He offers divine aid in its understanding. No study should therefore be undertaken without first calling on the Holy Spirit of God for His incomparable illumination.

• **Our Plan** is a survey course through the Bible. What does this mean? We aim to present the books, one by one, so that you may see them as a whole. First examine the book in its major divisions and overall message so that you may later examine the details more easily and efficiently. Our study might be likened to an arrival into a new city. First, you might climb a high building or neighboring mountain to chart the main divisions and intersecting streets. Later, you will more leisurely drive through and become acquainted with the shopping and residential areas and the people.

• **Be Assured** that the material you are now handling will live eternally. When great skyscrapers and giant bridges have crumbled into the dust of the centuries, the Word of God will still be as bright and shining as it is today.

Introduction

1. The Bible Is One Book

Seven marks attest this unity:
The Bible bears witness to one God
The Bible forms one continuous story
The Bible offers one system of prediction
The Bible progressively unfolds one system of truth
The Bible testifies to one redemption
The Bible has one great theme . . . Christ
The Bible shows perfect harmony in progressive unfolding

2. The Bible's Books Comprise Distinctive Groups:

Preparation . . . the Old Testament
Manifestation . . . the Four Gospels
Propagation . . . the Book of Acts
Explanation . . . the Epistles
Consumation . . . the Revelation

3. The Old Testament Suggests:

Books of Redemption: Genesis, Exodus, Leviticus, Numbers, Deuteronomy

Books of Organization: Joshua, Judges, Ruth, I & II Samuel, I & II Kings, I & II Chronicles, Ezra, Nehemiah, Esther

Books of Poetry: Job, Psalms, Proverbs, Ecclesiastes, Song of Solomon, Lamentations

Books of Sermons: Isaiah, Jeremiah, Ezekiel, Daniel, Hosea, Joel, Amos, Obadiah, Jonah, Micah, Nahum, Habakkuk, Zephaniah, Haggai, Zechariah, Malachi

4. The New Testament Suggests:

Books of Biography: Matthew, Mark, Luke, John
Books of History: Acts
Books of Doctrine (letters, too): Romans, Galatians, Hebrews

Books of Christian Living (letters): I & II Corinthians, I & II Timothy, Titus, I, II & III John

Books of Personal Letters: Ephesians, Colossians, I & II Thessalonians, Philippians, Philemon, James, I & II Peter, Jude

Book of Prophecy: Revelation

5. Relation of the Old Testament to the New Testament:

The New is in the Old contained,
The Old is by the New explained.
Truth enfolded in the Old,
Truth unfolded in the New.

6. The Bible Speaks of Itself:

As a mirror (James 1:25) to reveal our true condition

As a laver (Eph. 5:26) to cleanse us

As a lamp and light (Ps. 119:105) to guide us

As food—milk, bread, strong meat, honey (Heb. 5:12-14; Ps. 19:10)

As fine gold (Ps. 19:10) to enrich us

As fire, hammer, sword (Jer. 23:29; Heb. 4:12; Eph. 6:17) for life's warfare

As seed (James 1:18; I Pet. 1:23; Matt. 13:18-23) for the propagation of the Gospel message

7. Helps to Understanding:

Begin your study with the New Testament

Study plan: "Search" (John 5:39); "Meditate" (Ps. 1:2); "Compare" (I Cor. 2:13).

In reading, first read "synthetically" (book at a time), then read and study "analytically" (bit by bit).

Procure study aids: Bible Concordance, Bible Dictionary, Bible Commentary.

- Certain institutions and groups are found in the New Testament which are not described or authorized in the Old. These arose in the inter-testament period of 400 years.
- **The Sanhedrin:** The high council of the Jewish nation begun at the time of Ezra and Nehemiah for the purpose of reconstructing the religious life of the returning captives from Babylon. At the time of Christ it was composed of 70 members (no doubt from Num. 11:16, 17) mostly priests, Sadducean nobles, Pharisees, and Scribes. It was presided over by a high priest and exercises tremendous power of the Nation.
- **The Synagogue:** Synagogues arose at the time of the captivity in Babylon. Because the temple was destroyed and the nation scattered, there was desperate need for places where the people could be instructed and where they could worship. So these were local gatherings of the Jews, presided over by a board of elders. The Scriptures were publicly read and instruction was given to the young. After the captivity ended the synagogues persisted and were in time taken to countries where Jews were scattered.
- **The Pharisees:** In the third century before Christ, due largely to Alexandor's conquests, Greek culture and pagan worship were sweeping the known world. To combat this influence there was a reaction on the part of the God-fearing Jews to meet this onslaught of paganism and to preserve their national integrity and conformity to the Mosaic laws.

Born in a spirit of fervent patriotism and religious devotion, the Pharisees eventually developed into self-righteous and hypocritical formalists. In the time of Christ they were numerous, powerful and very influ-

ential. While for the most part their lives were exemplary, they were the strict legalists of the day. Christ had frequent conflicts with this group.

• **The Sadducees:** This sect arose about the same time as the Pharisees. These were more liberally minded Jews who favored the adoption of the prevailing Greek culture and customs. No doubt they were guided somewhat by secular considerations. They were a priestly clique but were irreligious. While not so numerous as the Pharisees, they nevertheless exercised great influence due to their wealth and position. They would be called today the religious rationalists. To a considerable extent they controlled the Sanhedrin in Christ's day.

•**The Scribes:** Originally Scribes were copyists of the Scriptures. This was a calling of great importance because of the value of the law in the lives of the people, and the absence of mechanical printing. They seemed to have originated during the Exile. Their work included the study and the interpretation of the Scriptures as well as the copying. Hence they became recognized authorities and their advice was sought on many matters. Some of them handed down decisions which became a sort of oral law. Others gathered schools about them. Scriptures sometimes speak of them as "lawyers." They worked closely with the Pharisees.

• **The Dispersion:** At the end of the Exile many Jews chose to remain in the lands where they were captives. So many, in fact, that there were more Jews living outside the land than in. Strong colonies of Jews arose in many lands and in the chief cities of the world. In every place they had their culture, their synagogues, and their Scriptures. At the time of Christ there were more than a million Jews living in Egypt alone. These Jews of the

Dispersion profoundly influenced the thought of many nations, while they in turn were influenced by the national life into which they had come. No doubt this was part of God's plan.

• **The Apocrypha:** This is the name given to some 14 books of outside writing appearing in some Bibles. The name itself means "spurious writings." They seem to have originated at the time of the writing of the Septuagint, a translation of the Hebrew Scriptures into the Greek language made about 250 B.C. in Alexandria supposedly by 70 scholars. These books, however, not found in the Hebrew Scriptures, were never accepted by the Hebrew authorities. So far as the New Testament is concerned, they are not quoted at all, nor referred to by Christ. Protestant scholars reject them as spurious and uninspired, while the Catholics due to the fact that their Latin version was largely based on the Septuagint, has included them.

Possibly based on actual happenings they add nothing to Bible doctrine.

OLD TESTAMENT

Genesis

1. STATISTICS

Name means "beginnings" or "originations;" writer is law-giver Moses (Exod. 17:14; Deut. 31:24); time of writing approximately 1500 B.C. Genesis is first of Pentateuch (meaning five books); place of writing, undoubtedly in wilderness. It is fourth largest book in the Bible; covers more than 2,500 years of human history.

2. THEME

Genesis depicts the first chapter of life. Here is the true story of how all things began. Here is the stately portal to the grand structure of the Holy Scriptures. Here is man's introduction to the magnificence of God Almighty. Here is the sad story of the introduction of sin.

3. OUTLINE

Creation (1, 2)	Deluge (6-9)	Isaac (21-27)
Fall (3, 4)	Nations (10, 11)	Jacob (25-36)
Patriarchs (5)	Abraham (12-25)	Joseph (37-50)

4. SPECIAL CHARACTERISTICS

Here is a book of simple, direct honesty. There is no hesitation, no supposition, no apology. These are God's facts.

The opening verse is a masterpiece of all literature.

Countless volumes have been written about these ten words. Where is another such statement?

Genesis is unique for its portrayal of beginnings. Everything we know had its start here.

The book is eclectic. Choosing to tell mainly of the history of one family, Abraham; one nation, Israel, it passes by the story of many nations.

5. OUTSTANDING TEACHINGS

God had no beginning. He pre-existed all creation.

The fact of sin is a solemn reality. The entire human race is included in the Fall.

God is greatly concerned with man's redemption. His first act after the Fall was to provide coats of skins.

A horrible example of the depravity of man is the cold-blooded murder of Abel.

Mankind, left to himself for several thousand years, became so depraved there was no remedy left except death for all (Flood) and a new start with Noah.

The judgment of the Tower of Babel is a logical answer to the problem of where the nations of the world began.

The God of eternity found pleasure in the fellowship of a man made of earthy clay. Abraham became the "friend of God" on the basis of his faith (chap. 15).

Joseph is the Bible's greatest type of the coming Saviour in more than 100 different analogies.

6. INTERESTING FEATURES

Genesis 1:1 thoroughly refutes: atheism, pantheism, polytheism, materialism and agnosticism.

It is possible that 25 million people perished in the Flood.

Genesis does not tell the date of creation.

7. KEY TO UNDERSTANDING

Genesis is cold, sober fact. Read it and believe it at face value. Recognize that all truth found later in the Bible has its roots here.

Exodus

1. STATISTICS

Some 30 years elapsed between Genesis and Exodus. The Children of Israel increased exceedingly to 3,000,000 souls. A change in the reigning dynasty sentenced them to cruel slavery. Exodus tells the story of their "going out." Writer is Moses (24:4) and time covered is about 80 years from his birth.

2. THEME

The theme is threefold: the faithfulness, the power, the wisdom of God. First, God was faithful to His promises to Abraham, Isaac and Jacob. So, by His power, He opened the iron gates of Egypt. When Sinai was reached, God provided an infinitely wise law by which the Children of Israel were to live.

3. OUTLINE

Preparation for
  Deliverance (1-13)
Journey to Sinai (14-19)
Laws given (20-24)
Tabernacle (25-27; 30, 31)

Priesthood (28, 29)
Idolatry (32, 33)
Covenant (34)
Tabernacle erection (35-40)

4. SPECIAL CHARACTERISTICS

This book breathes the presence of God. He was aware of the plight of His people and did something about it.

Exodus is particularly the book of a great servant of God, Moses. Here is a man who talked with God face to face.

The Mosaic Law is God's highest for His people. It is heavenly wisdom simplified for earthly living.

The Israelites' journey to the Promised Land has become a giant object lesson for the Christian life today.

Here began the sad story (chap. 32) of man's failure which was repeated continually in Israel's history.

5. OUTSTANDING TEACHINGS

Moses' life was divided into three periods: 40 years in schools of Egypt; 40 years in school of God (tending sheep in the desert); 40 years in service. At the end of his life he was still strong and able (Deut. 34:7).

The ten plagues were directed against the Egyptian government, but were also a demonstration against the gods of Egypt. For instance, the first two plagues showed Jehovah superior to the god of the Nile; the third against the earth god Seb and the priests who could not officiate with lice upon them.

The Israelites could not be delivered until they came "under the blood" of the Passover. This is the central fact in God's relationship and a continual reminder of sin and need for cleansing.

God immediately took up His residence among His people. They could see the sign of His presence in the pillar of fire and cloud.

The Ten Commandments are given as an epitome of the law, easily taught and easily remembered.

6. INTERESTING FEATURES

Exodus begins the original "Pilgrim's Progress" for an estimated 3 million people.

How much manna was required for 40 years? (16:15, 21)

Note how meticulous God is about details (Heb. 8:5)

7. KEY TO UNDERSTANDING

Exodus is geographically and historically accurate: believe it entirely. However, its main value today is to take the experiences, trials, and deliverances and apply them to the Christian life.

Leviticus

1. STATISTICS

Third in series of five (Pentateuch) by the same writer,

Moses (Rom. 10:5); name means "pertaining to or concerning the Levites;" these were members of the Tribe of Levi, especially set aside for the work of God; time written, at Sinai; time involved, one month or less; type of book, possibly an instruction manual for priests.

2. THEME

In view of the infinite holiness of God, how can sinful man approach and walk before Him? There is an approach and it is by way of sacrifice. There is a life and it is by way of separation. All this is taught by sacrifices, feasts, tabernacle and laws.

3. OUTLINE

Offerings (1-7)
Priests' consecration (8,9)
Nadab and Abihu (10)
Purity of life (11-15)
Day of Atonement (16, 17)

Warnings of sin (18-.22)
Feasts described (23-25)
Obedience (26)
Vows, tithes (27)

4. SPECIAL CHARACTERISTICS

God counts worship important. To fail is to sin (10:2, Exod. 20:5).

The number "seven" is emphasized: the seventh day, the seventh year, the year of Jubilee (7 x 7), etc.

Leviticus named specific horrible sins. Frankness was necessary because these things were being practiced by iniquitous neighbors.

Priesthood was definitely a part of Old Testament system. In the New, Christ is High Priest, all believers priests (I Pet. 2:9).

5. OUTSTANDING TEACHINGS

The priests were an integral part of God's plan for Israel. Provision was made for their support through portions of the offerings, and through tithes. The rest of the Levites were assistants to the priests. They became teachers, scribes, musicians, judges, officers.

God sent swift death of two sons of Aaron (10:1, 2).

Their sin was that of professional presumption. They entered where they should not, and with fire not taken from the altar. God cannot allow carelessness in divine things.

God required capital punishment for many crimes. Many offenses were punishable with death including: murder, kidnapping, negligence, cursing a parent, idolatry, etc. (see chaps. 19, 20).

In 19:18 we have one of the high points of the law. Generally considered to be a New Testament truth, the Israelite was commanded, "Love thy neighbor as thyself."

Tremendous wisdom was exhibited in the Law. Many provisions reveal that God desired His children to love Him and to love one another. When they did this, He would care for their temporal needs.

The great day of the year was the Day of Atonement (chap. 16). At this time the high priest entered the Holy of Holies to make atonement for the sins of the people.

6. INTERESTING FEATURES

The yearly feasts partook of the nature of holidays. Everyone had three vacations yearly, an entire year off every seven, and once in a lifetime the year of Jubilee was tremendous rejoicing.

Slavery was not forbidden but hedged with humane considerations.

Every 50 years all the land reverted to its original owners.

7. KEY TO UNDERSTANDING

If God gave a law to us today, this would be it. All its provisions are divinely suited to human needs. Some of your greatest blessings here are to relate these earthly laws to spiritual truths, as the Day of Atonement represents Calvary.

Numbers

1. STATISTICS

Moses is the writer; Numbers is fourth in his series of five books; written about 1500 B.C.; covers approximately 40 years; key verse 33:1; takes its name from two numberings of the people; tells of progress from Sinai to borders of the Promised Land.

2. THEME

Numbers is a book of instructions and action; its instruction is like Leviticus, its action like Exodus. Essentially, it tells the story of the journeyings of the Israelites from Sinai to Kadesh and after 38 years of useless wanderings, on to the plains of Moab by the borders of the land.

3. OUTLINE

Three main divisions: (1) Laws given while at Sinai (1-10); (2) Journey to Kadesh (11-21); (3) Camping at Moab (22-36).

4. SPECIAL CHARACTERISTICS

Numbers tells of a 40-day journey which took 40 years.

It is a book of "numberings" but also "murmurings" (7 times).

Our admiration of the man Moses rises to great heights. Here is truly a spiritual giant (14:11-20).

This was a case where the majority were dead wrong. They discounted the fact that God would be with them. (13:26-33).

Two census counts were taken, one at the beginning of the 38 years of wandering and the other at the close. Result: no gain whatsoever. 1200 men died monthly in the wandering years.

Balaam's doctrine (Rev. 2:14; Num. 25:1-8) of fraternization with the world is exceedingly dangerous to the people of God. Here God slew 24,000.

5. OUTSTANDING TEACHINGS

The 38 years of shame God counts a blank. There is no record, no progress, no increase. God passes them by.

God was grieved at the unreasoning unbelief of the people (Ps. 95:10), but nevertheless turned the years into preparation for the future. Boys grew to men, ready and trained for the rigors of war.

One of the greatest types (object lessons) of the Bible is in 21:5-10. Our Lord used this as an illustration in his conversation with Nicodemus (John 3:14).

The command to destroy the inhabitants of Canaan was a divine one (33:51-56). God's love has teeth in it. It would have been impossible for Israel to be pure in the midst of such wickedness.

Balaam was an example of a servant of God among the Gentiles. His life was a warning to others of God's servants. For the love of earthly gain, he sold out. The book records his untimely death (31:8).

It pays to serve God faithfully. Consider Caleb and Joshua who were allowed to live while 600,000 others died.

6. INTERESTING FEATURES

A beautiful intercessory prayer (14:11-20).
One of the loveliest benedictions in the Bible (6:24-26).
God keeps books (14:22).
Word "number" used 125 times in this book.
Israel wins a battle with Midian without a single casualty.
A lot of quail in 11:31.
A miracle in the botanical realm (17:8).

7. KEY TO UNDERSTANDING

You could change the whole miserable character of this disappointing book if you could substitute "trust" for unbelief. Let this be a lesson to all of us.

Deuteronomy

1. STATISTICS

Deuteronomy is the fifth book in the Pentateuch; writer

Moses who did not complete it until just before his death; time of writing 1500 B.C.; Actual time covered is one month, but review is made of past 40 years; place of writing at southeast entrance into Promised Land; key verses, 11:26-28; name means "second" or "reiterated" Law, i.e., stating the Law with a view of its usage in the land.

2. THEME

Deuteronomy was Moses' magnificent valedictory. It looked back over the important events of the past 40 years, and forward to the glorious victories of the future. The underlying strain concerned God's faithfulness and the challenge was to trust Him and go forward.

3. OUTLINE

Review and warnings (1-4)　Possible blessings and
Reminders of the Cov-　　 curses (27-30)
　enant (5-11)
Warnings about future　　Moses' farewell (31-34)
　(12-26)

4. SPECIAL CHARACTERISTICS

The entire book is composed of Moses' words. Speeches were made eloquent by the Spirit of God for Moses had admitted he could not speak (Exod. 4:10-13).

As literature, the book is magnificent, classed with Genesis, Psalms and Isaiah.

The writer's poetic nature is demonstrated in his "national anthem" of chapter 32. See also Exod. 15; Ps. 90.

There are two great prophetic sections: 18:15-19; 28-30.

Emphasis of the book is a stern review of moral laws. Temptations were just ahead. A new generation had grown up.

Nowhere in the Pentateuch until here do we read of the love of God. Note here the emphasis: 4:37; 7:7, 8; 10:15.

The word "remember" is necessarily prominent, occurring 18 times.

5. OUTSTANDING TEACHINGS

The central chapter is 27. Here is condensed for public recitation an epitome of the Lord's requirements.

The Decalogue (10 commandments) is repeated in chapter 5. Most of the present host would dimly remember the "thunderings and lightnings" of Sinai 40 years before.

The importance of daily, ceaseless training of children is emphasized in chapter 6.

The necessity of complete extermination of the wicked people of the land of Canaan is detailed in chapter 7. The reason was so that God's people might not be corrupted.

Moses was not allowed to enter the land because of his sin (32:51); yet fourteen centuries later we do find him in the land at the scene of the transfiguration of Christ (Matt. 17:3).

Provisions were made for the continual reading of the Law (31:9-13) after Moses' death, also, for the recording of the Law in plaster, on Mt. Ebal "very plainly" (27:2-4; Josh. 8:30-32). When the nation heeded the Law they prospered. When they neglected it, they suffered.

6. INTERESTING FEATURES

Specific military rules in chapter 20.

Last chapter of book (34) probably written by Joshua.

God believes in punishment, but not in bitter cruelty (25:1-3).

A good test for false prophets (18:20-22).

Chapter 33 is similar to Gen. 49

Read and note the spiritual foresight of Moses as he described the centuries of wandering of the Jews in 28:63-68.

7. KEY TO UNDERSTANDING

You will best understand Deuteronomy after you have read the first four books. Then, in your imagination stand with Moses and look back, and forward. This book lives!

Joshua

1. STATISTICS

Writer, Joshua (24:26); written abut 1425 B.C.; time covered about 25 years; type of book, history; Joshua lived to be 110; key verse 1:8; key thought, possession.

2. THEME

Joshua is a book of progress, conquest, possession, and systematic division of the land. With a new leader, there were new experiences, new victories, new attainments and new problems. But God's guidance, God's power, and God's encouragement were the same. Joshua is the chief personage.

3. OUTLINE

Conquest (1-12)   Joshua's farewell (23,24)
Settlement of the land
  (13-22)

4. SPECIAL CHARACTERISTICS

Joshua is a book of action and corresponds to the challenges, victories and thrills of the Christian life.

These events in Joshua demonstrate great principles: the rite of circumcision at Gilgal (chap. 5), the necessity for separation; the memorials (chap. 4), a sign of remembrance of God's miracles.

Joshua's dependence upon the books of Moses was demonstrated: Compare Josh. 14:1-4 with Num. 34:13, 14; Josh. 13:17 with Num. 32:37; Josh. 21 with Num. 35.

God's man, Moses, was gone, but God's work went on under God's new leader, Joshua.

Here is a commander, Joshua, who was evidently reared in the brick factories, or iron foundries of Egypt.

5. OUTSTANDING TEACHINGS

The fact that God goes before His people is demonstrated in the fear He had put into the hearts of the Canaanites preparatory to the conquest (2:10, 11).

The unbelievable grace of God is shown in the inclusion of Rahab, a harlot, into the Messianic line of Christ (Matt. 1:5).

While the land had been already "given" to Israel (Gen. 15:18-21), still it was necessary that they go in and possess it. As they did God gave the victory.

The slaughter of the Canaanites (6:21; 10:28) was by God's direct command. This was absolutely necessary to cleanse the land for the occupation of God's chosen people, and entirely justifiable, for God had given 400 extra years for their repentance (Gen. 15:16).

Victory at Jericho was by complete observance of God's directions, defeat at Ai was due to disobedience, and that of one man.

The Tabernacle was set up at Shiloh for the gathering place of the Tribes to worship the Lord. Later, David made Jerusalem the religious center of the people.

The vindication of the minority report of the spies (Num. 14:6-10) was amply demonstrated in the complete conquest of the land.

The distribution "by lot" (Num. 33:54) evidently allowed God's hand to be present and recognized in the tribal divisions.

The miracle of the sun standing still and the great hailstones in the battle of Gibeon was entirely in keeping with the events which had been happening since Israel left Egypt.

6. INTERESTING FEATURES

Three campaigns result in seven nations with 31 kings defeated by Israel and Joshua (chap. 12).

Joshua's name appears in the Tel el Amarna tablets found in Egypt.

Jesus was baptized 1400 years later, probably near where Joshua crossed the Jordan.

7. KEY TO UNDERSTANDING

God's people made great advances under the leadership of a man named Joshua. God's people today may do the same under our Joshua (Jesus). Take this book literally, but do not fail to apply its spiritual lessons to your own life.

Judges

1. STATISTICS

Writer possibly the prophet, Samuel; time covered approximately 305 years; key verse, 17:6; key thought, disorganization and mis-government; key characteristics, unbelief and fickleness on the part of the people; type of book, history.

2. THEME

Judges is a tersely written account of repeated spiritual failures on the part of Israel. The period may be comprehended as: apostasy, punishment, repentance, deliverance. The root of the problem is countenanced idolatry introduced by pagan neighbors. The judges were really deliverers, raised up by God for the emergency, who stayed to "judge."

3. OUTLINE

Reason for judges
(1:1-3:4)
(1:1-3:4)
Story of 12 judges
(3:5-16:31)

Resultant instances of
anarchy (17-21)

4. SPECIAL CHARACTERISTICS

Joshua is a book of victory; Judges a book of defeats.

There were seven apostasies, seven oppressions by seven nations, seven deliverances.

While faith and obedience pulled down the walls of Jericho, unbelief and disobedience enslaved Israel for 300 years.

The divine estimation of the cause is given in 2:11-19. Read in connection 21:25.

Much is learned from the omissions of the book. There is no mention of the Tabernacle, only once is the High Priest named (20:28), no reference to reading the Law of God, no expressions of praise to God for His continued goodness.

Emphasis is on the tribes, not the united nation.

In Judges, God seems to stand and wait as the Israelites demonstrate their inability to independently care for themselves.

5. OUTSTANDING TEACHINGS

The sin of Israel in Judges was rooted in the failure to carry out completely the instructions of God (Deut. 7:1-6). So the pagans in their midst became a snare and temptation for them to forsake the true God and to serve idolatrous gods.

The judges who God raised up were not men of exceptional ability as Moses and Joshua. They performed their part and died. Evidently, there was no line of succession. Nor was there any expressed desire on Israel's part for a great leader for the nation. Both men and tribes seemed intent only on personal success or possessions.

The greatest of the judges was Gideon. He was called at a time of national emergency. His recruited army of 32,000 was whittled down to a pitiful 300 and then given no weapons. But never in all history was there a greater victory. Gideon's exploits are referred to in Psalm 83:9, 10; Isaiah 9:4; 10:26; Hebrews 11:32. His "fleece" episode is an encouragement to all God's children.

Samson's victories were all personal. By himself he injected terror into Philistia and courage into Israel. But he lacked the statesmanship of Samuel or the spiritual apperception of David. His great problem was to conquer himself, his appetites and passions. Yet he had faith in God and is immortalized in Hebrews 11:32.

6. INTERESTING FEATURES

We might call Judges the "dark ages" of the Israelitish

people.

A sad recital of "neither did's" is in 1:27-36.

Jephthah's vow led to the sacrifice of his daughter.

Deborah's song (chap. 5) is a beautiful song of victory.

Two great women, Deborah and Jael, inspire men for victory.

7. KEY TO UNDERSTANDING

Here is overwhelming proof (seven times) that children of God just cannot live successfully by "doing what is right in their own eyes." We must look to God, and rely upon the instruments of grace He has given: Bible, prayer, worship, leadership.

Ruth

1. STATISTICS

Ruth, a pastoral idyl taking place in the time of the Judges (approx. 1325 B.C.); time covered, about ten years; writer, Samuel, the prophet; key thought, "Redemption;" key verse 4:14.

2. THEME

While the nation disobeyed God and was punished, still God was wonderfully faithful to individuals who called upon Him in their need. An "outsider" Ruth, who sought the Lord with her whole heart, illustrates the grace of God which not only made up the deficit caused by sin, but exalted her to an unbelievably high place of privilege and honor.

3. OUTLINE

Ruth deciding (1)   Ruth resting (3)

Ruth serving (2)   Ruth rewarded (4)

4. SPECIAL CHARACTERISTICS

Highly typical: Boaz typifies Christ, Ruth the Church,

Moab the world, Bethlehem the fellowship of God, etc.

Moab, an idolatrous nation, worshiped Chemosh, sacrificing children.

Moab and Israel had slight physical relationship. Moabites were descendants of the incestuous union of Lot (Abraham's nephew) and his own daughter (Gen. 19:33-37).

The fields of Boaz were immediately adjacent to the shepherds' fields (Luke 2:8) of Bethlehem.

This little book was ofttimes read at the Feast of Pentecost as a picture of domestic life and love in a time of anarchy and trouble.

5. OUTSTANDING TEACHINGS

The central lesson is that only trouble results from leaving the Lord's land (Bethlehem) and that blessing will not come again until there is repentance and return.

The Law completely shut out the Moabite from a participation in the blessing of Israel (Deut. 23:3). Here, however, is the operation of the grace of God which transcends the curse, and lifts Ruth to immeasurable heights of privilege, placing her in the Messianic line (Matt. 1:5).

Boaz was the son of Rahab, the Jericho harlot (Josh. 2:1; Matt. 1:5). Thus David, the great-grandson of a Moabite and great great-grandson of a Canaanite, further demonstrated the grace of God.

Ruth's lovely confession to Naomi (1:16, 17) is one of the grandest examples of literary jewels the world possesses. This fell from the lips of a heathen maiden who evidently saw in the family of her deceased husband the real goal of living.

The Levirate law known as the Kinsman-Redeemer, finds its most outstanding example here. The law had provided that when a man died, and there were no children, the brother should take the wife and raise up children for his deceased brother (Deut. 25:5-10).

Also, if the property of the dead brother must be sold

for any reason, it was to be redeemed by a near kinsman so as to preserve the inheritance. The redeemer must, of course, be a kinsman, and must be able to redeem, which meant paying the just demands in full. Boaz fulfilled this perfectly and became a type of Christ, our Kinsman-Redeemer, who rescued us from our lost condition by fully paying the price of our sin (I Pet. 1:18, 19; Gal. 3:13).

6. INTERESTING FEATURES

Note excellent labor relations between Boaz and his workmen (2:4). The incident (3:1-11) is not indelicate, but merely a custom of presenting the claims inherent in the kinsman problem.

7. KEY TO UNDERSTANDING

You will understand this book more perfectly as you put yourself in the place of Ruth; see Boaz as Christ your Redeemer, and the marriage as your salvation.

I Samuel

1. STATISTICS

Writers, Samuel (10:25), possibly Nathan and Gad (I Chron. 29:29); time involved, about 120 years; key thought, "kingdom;" key verse, 12:13; type of book, history; principal character, Saul.

2. THEME

This is mainly the story of the rise and fall of King Saul, introduced by the prophet Samuel, and followed on the throne by David.

3. OUTLINE

Samuel as judge (1-7)   David persecuted (16-30)
Saul begins to reign (8-15) Saul's defeat, death (28, 31)

4. SPECIAL CHARACTERISTICS

This book begins the line of writing prophets. From this time the prophet rather than the priest is conspicuous in Israel.

Samuel was a child of faith and prayer. His father was a Levite (I Chron. 6:27, 28), and before his birth he was dedicated to the Lord. Hannah's lovely prayer of thanksgiving seems somewhat similar to the great magnificat of Mary (Luke 1:46-55).

Moses had foreseen and predicted the coming of the kingship (Deut. 17:14, 15).

Samuel was a "circuit rider" as a judge (7:15-17).

The "schools of the prophets" were evidently introduced under Samuel (10:5, 10; 19:20; II Kings 2:3-5).

Samuel's ministry included that of being a "king-maker."

5. OUTSTANDING TEACHINGS

Eli and Samuel were both men of godly integrity. However, evidently being busy in the service of God, they neglected their own sons with tragic results (2:12-17; 8:3-5).

The ark of the covenant was a blessing to God's people, but a curse to the enemies of the Lord (chap. 5).

Saul was the people's choice for king. In the natural, he possessed many qualifications. He started well, and had he continued, his story would have been entirely different. His great deficiency was a lack of spiritual appreciation.

Saul's errors were those common to rulers: (1) impatience as he waited for Samuel (13:8-14); impetuosity in the flush of victory where he made a rash vow (chap. 14); disobedience to the clear command of God and acting in his own self-well (chap. 15). Along with these was a resultant insane jealousy he had for David. All of these human frailties might have been counterbalanced by simple and sincere dependence upon God, who gives to rulers their special abilities.

David is introduced here. Undoubtedly he is the most colorful figure in the whole Bible. He was a rich combination of soldier, statesman, shepherd, musician, singer, poet. His magnificent victory over Goliath was a demonstration of the courage that may accompany simple faith in God.

Two of David's inner qualities stand out boldly. His deep and sincere love for his friend, Jonathan, and his patience in waiting God's time to ascend the throne for which he had already been anointed.

Apparently the appearance of Samuel in the home of the witch of Endor was genuine for it greatly frightened even the witch. Witchcraft, of course, had been strictly forbidden by the Law and this was a sad commentary on the spiritual status of Saul's heart (Lev. 20:27; Deut. 18:10-12).

6. INTERESTING FEATURES

First and Second Samuel were originally one book.

Goliath's armor weighed more than 150 pounds; his spearhead alone was 20 pounds. It is questionable if David at this time weighed 150 pounds.

Many of the psalms of David were written at this time.

7. KEY TO UNDERSTANDING

As in all the Books of God, the divine Author selects only material which is for our edification. The key is the contrast of the inner qualities of Saul and David, and the resultant accomplishments. Apply this to your own heart.

II Samuel

1. STATISTICS

Writers, Nathan, a prophet, and Gad, a seer (I Chron. 27:24; 29:29); time covered, about 40 years; type of book, history; key thought, full establishment of kingdom; key verse, 7:16; key character, David.

2. THEME

The story of David as king: his reign in Hebron, his coronation over the entire nation, his military exploits and victories, his grievous sin and the sad train of consequential punishments.

3. OUTLINE

David at Hebron (1-4)   Many conquests (8-10)
David king over all Israel   David's sin and repentance
   (5-24)   (11, 12)
Ark restored (6, 7)   Absalom's rebellion (13-19)
                               David's last days (20-24)

4. SPECIAL CHARACTERISTICS

The frankness in describing David's sin is proof of Divine authorship of the book.

Here is the height of the kingdom (see Gen. 15:18-21).

One of David's psalms is chapter 22.

A great military leader inspired talented followers (23).

Psalms written from his experiences: his flight from Jerusalem (Psa. 3, 4), his song of military victory (Psa. 30, 60), his sin (Psa. 51).

5. OUTSTANDING TEACHINGS

David's greatest commendation was to be called "a man after God's own heart" (I Sam. 13:14). How could this be, in view of his great sin? The answer is his whole-souled repentance. Whatever else, he had a heart for God. His many psalms reveal this.

Not only was David gracious and forgiving, but he utterly discouraged vindictiveness, and went out of his way to be kind to Saul's kin (chap. 9).

God's covenant with David regarding a perpetual throne (chap. 7) is one of the Bible's greatest chapters. (See also: Psa. 89:27-29; Jer. 33:20, 21, 25; Luke 1:30-33).

David's great capacity for worship evidenced in his

bringing the ark of the covenant to Jerusalem and establishing ritual and order of the temple service as soon as the land was quiet from war.

God forgave David's sin, but its consequences followed him all his life.Murder and adultery occurred again and again in his family. Sin is truly a damnable thing.

6. INTERESTING FEATURES

Watercourse ("gutter" 5:8) is still seen in Jerusalem.

Jerusalem was one of the most easily defended capital cities of the ancient world.

Some amazing records are marked by David's mighty men (chap. 23).

Absalom's vanity (luxurious head of hair) became his downfall.

7. KEY TO UNDERSTANDING

How can one today be a "man after God's own heart?" It was surely not in his sin, but in his whole-souled sorrow and repentance that David could be thus named.

I Kings

1. STATISTICS

Writer, Jeremiah, according to tradition; note similarity of II Kings 25 and Jer. 39; 52; covers 120 years, key thought, kingdom glory and decline; key verse, 2:12; key characters, Solomon, Elijah; Type of book, history.

2. THEME

Following David's death, Solomon became king, ruled well, built the temple but eventually made some serious mistakes. At his death the kingdom was divided and a great prophet, Elijah, came on the scene.

3. OUTLINE

David's counsel and .death (1, 2)	Division and early Kings (12-16)
Solomon's magnificence and temple (3-11)	Elijah emerges (17-19)
	King Ahab's story (20-22)

4. SPECIAL CHARACTERISTICS

Books of Kings present the political aspect of the time while Chronicles present the priestly aspect of the same period.

Other existing books referred to by sacred writer: book of Acts of Solomon; History of Nathan; History of Gad; Visions of Iddo.

Solomon was a colorful figure to describe. He wrote 3000 proverbs and 1005 songs, and besides was an authority on botany and zoology.

The second half of the book deals mainly with the prophet Elijah.

5. OUTSTANDING FEATURES

Solomon's reign began in splendor as in deep humility he asked for wisdom. He received wisdom, wealth and honor. The downfall of the world's wisest man came in his failure to follow God's admonitions.

His reign prefigures the millennial kingdom when "the earth shall be filled with the knowledge of the Lord as the waters cover the sea."

His unique wisdom did not save him from the idolatry introduced by his heathen wives. Unlike David, he did not show penitence and confess his sin. At his death, his kingdom was seething with unrest.

Rehoboam's foolish decision split the Tribes into two nations which remained through the period of the captivity. There were a few of the kings of Judah who followed the Lord, but for the most part the picture of both kingdoms was a sad one. The strongest impression is the long-suffering patience of God.

Elijah, one of two remarkable prophets in the Northern

Kingdom, first appeared as a grown man, facing King Ahab with flaming reproof. A strange supernatural atmosphere surrounded him. He was like a lion, strong, stern. He performed miracles and lived as an ascetic. He was God's man for the hour.

To keep Israel from religious pilgrimages to Jerusalem, Jeroboam erected two golden calves to worship in Bethel and Dan. He became a synonym for sin in Israel's history. Again and again following his name is the phrase "who made Israel to sin."

6. INTERESTING FEATURES

There were 19 kings (9 dynasties) in Israel; 20 kings (1 dynasty) in Judah.

Solomon had extensive stables (9:15, 16; 10:26, 28) at Megiddo.

A three-word description of the kings following Solomon would be: idolatry, immorality and bloodshed.

7. KEY TO UNDERSTANDING

Study the life of Solomon and ask: Why did this king fail when he had started so magnificently? Make a list of the kings of Judah and Israel and you will see the size of the grace of God.

II Kings

1. STATISTICS

Writer, probably Jeremiah; time of writing, 900 B.C.; key thought, decline of kingdom; key verse, 17:9; time covered, about 300 years; type of book, history.

2. THEME

A continuation of the decline of the kingdom period, including the inevitable captivity of the northern tribes, later, the southern. Miracle-ministry of the prophet, Elisha, is prominent.

3. OUTLINE

Decline and final capti- Decline and final captivity
vity of Israel (1-17)   of Judah (18-25)

4. SPECIAL CHARACTERISTICS

History of man's inexcusable failures and God's immeasurable love.

This was one of three periods of miracles; others were during the life of Moses and during Christ's earthly ministry.

One figure is predominant—Elisha the prophet, successor to Elijah. The former was opposite of the latter in every respect, yet was God's man for the hour.

5. OUTSTANDING TEACHINGS

Elisha asked for a double portion of Elijah's spirit (2:9). There are just twelve miracles recorded for him, six for Elijah. The affected nations and individuals, with whom God is concerned: The Syrian siege (chaps. 6, 7), the Shunammite's son (4:8-37).

Two great lessons in Naaman's healing: the connecting link provided by the captive girl and the fact that God allowed His truth to be known to pagan nations as well as to His chosen people.

The fulfillment awaited God's time, but frightful judgment inexorable came to the wicked Jezebel (9:10, 30-37), perhaps the most wicked woman pictured in the Bible.

The Messianic line hangs on a thread, the life of a six-year-old, Joash (11:1-3).

Prayers reveal inner character. The inner heart of King Hezekiah is seen from his earnest prayers (19:14-19, 20:1-3).

A complete account of God's reasons for allowing Israel to go into captivity is given (17:7-23).

God answers Hezekiah's prayer for extended life, but in this time Manasseh, the most frightfully wicked king of all, was born to him (chaps. 20, 21). How much better God's way.

The reading of God's Word brings results (22:11-14; 23:1-27).

6. INTERESTING FEATURES

Elijah a "fire" prophet, miracles during his life and his homegoing.

Solomon's temple completely destroyed (25:8-10).

The captivity of Judah in four installments.

Reappearance of Elijah in Matt. 17:1-3, at Transfiguration.

7. KEY TO UNDERSTANDING

God forestalled judgment upon His people for many years, but it finally had to fall. Had there been a genuine repentance and revival they would have been spared. That same long-suffering patience is seen in God's dealing with the unsaved today.

I Chronicles

1. STATISTICS

Writer, presumably Ezra, scribe and priest (II Chron. 36:22 and Ezra 1:1, 2); time of writing 500 B.C.; key thought, kingdom history from sacred standpoint; key verse, 29:26; type of book, history and genealogical records; chronicles means "word of days," "journal" or "record."

2. THEME

A condensed history, beginning with Adam and ending with captivity of Jewish nation (including II Chronicles), with emphasis on the reign of David, Israel's greatest king.

3. OUTLINE
Genealogical records   Reign of David (11-29)
(1-10)

4. SPECIAL CHARACTERISTICS

Book is part of a recapitulation of II Samuel but with a different purpose in mind. Writer was concerned with an accurate statistical record for the time in which he was writing and for the future.

Books of Samuel and Kings (102 chapters) cover 585 years of pure history. Prophets are important; kings of both nations are named, special emphasis on prominent ones. Two books of Chronicles (65 chapters) cover 460 years of religious history. Priests are important; they tell only of the good kings of Judah.

Whatever has to do with the temple, purity of its worship, regularity of its services, its preservation or restoration is emphasized. The attitude of the kings to the King of kings is shown to be the key to national success.

The ministry of music is fully set forth; the duties of the Levites were designated and the priesthood was organized into 24 courses. Doorkeepers and treasurers were authorized as well as David's civil servants.

Public worship was given special attention. God was seen to be greatly interested in regular assembling of the people to honor Him. It was necessary that there be instruction as to how to make such worship acceptable.

5. OUTSTANDING TEACHINGS

While in the books of Samuel and Kings we found wars, idolatries, and offenses; in this book are deliverances, repentances, and reformations. In the former, idolatry appears as treason against the king, in the latter, the apostasy was against God.

Four great deliverances in (I & II) Chronicles and in each case victory was by God's hand.

David had many valuable friends (chaps. 11, 12). They were described as "expert in war, with all instruments of war;" with "faces like the faces of lions."

They were "as swift as roes (deer) upon the montains" and they could "use both the right hand and the left."

David was given the honor of preparing materials for the temple which was to be built by Solomon (chap. 22). He collected vast stores of gold, silver, and building materials. The estimate of the value is from two to five billion dollars. David said concerning the temple it "must be exceeding magnifical" (v. 5).

The great Davidic covenant (II Sam. 7) was reiterated in I Chron. 17:7-15. This is one of God's unconditional agreements with Israel. (See also Psa. 89:20-37).

The ark of His covenant had been in Kirjath-jearim for 20 years (I Sam. 7:2); then in the house of Obed-edom for three months. Now in grand triumphal procession, David brought it to a tent prepared for it in Jerusalem (chap. 15).

6. INTERESTING FEATURES

Uzza's death came as a result of doing the right thing, in the wrong way (13:9, 10).

David refused to give an offering to the Lord which had cost him nothing (21:22-26).

7. KEY TO UNDERSTANDING

Repetition means emphasis. What God has restated in Chronicles should be noted carefully.

II Chronicles

1. STATISTICS

Writer, probably Ezra, scribe-priest; time of writing about 500 B.C.; covers period of about 400 years; type of book, history; key thought, kingdom of Judah (emphasis on good kings); key verse, 15:2; key character, Solomon.

2. THEME

Solomon, his temple and his glory, and the kings which

followed him. Emphasis on miracles God accomplished through kings of Judah.

3. OUTLINE

Solomon's reign, temple, fame (1-9)

Judah's kings, wars, victories (10-36)

Babylonian captivity, restoration (36)

4. SPECIAL CHARACTERISTICS

Building, splendor and dedication of the temple most important.

Little mentioned of sin and failure. Righteous kings and their acts are emphasized. Religious side is uppermost.

Ezra, a Levite, writes from that standpoint. When the split came between the tribes at the time of Rehoboam, practically all the Levites moved to the Southern Kingdom where they ministered.

Undoubtedly written late, possibly one of the latest, since other books are mentioned (I Chron. 29:29).

As pure history this book is of less value than Samuel and Kings. Most valuable as religious interpretation of history by an eyewitness of much of it.

5. OUTSTANDING TEACHINGS

It was the added blessings of God that Solomon abused, which led to his downfall.

Temple was built after the general pattern of the tabernacle in the wilderness, with parts just twice the dimensions. Some 30,000 Jews and 150,000 Canaanites labored 7½ years without the sound of a hammer during its assembling.

The altar of burnt offering is thought to have stood on the rock now enclosed in the Mohammedan "Dome of the Rock" which was the traditional spot of Abraham's offering of Isaac (Gen. 22).

Jehoshaphat reigned for 25 years and "sought the Lord in all things." He began a system of public instruction in the homes of the people as priests and Levites taught the law of God. His courts of justice throughout the land, with a court of appeals at Jerusalem, greatly strengthened righteous living (chaps. 17-20).

Hezekiah inherited a badly disorganized kingdom but started out with a great reformation. He cleansed and restored the temple, kept the passover, and "trusted in God." He also leaned heavily on Isaiah.

The last kings were tragic in their wickedness, until there was no remedy. Zedekiah was taken in chains to Babylon where he died. Jerusalem and the great temple were utterly demolished.

6. INTERESTING FEATURES

God Himself was the architect of the temple (I Chron. 29:19).

Shishak's sarcophagus of pure gold has been found, possibly made of some of Solomon's gold (12:9).

Josiah had one of the most remarkable reigns in Judah's history. When only 8 years of age he sought the Lord. In his eighteenth year of reign he found the Book which brought a great reformation.

Note similarity in 36:22, 23 and Ezra 1:1-3.

7. KEY TO UNDERSTANDING

The key to national success is a complete and continual recognition of God's place. Only when He is reverenced, worshiped, and His commandments observed, can there be true prosperity. You will want to take God's position as you "observe" the happenings of II Chronicles.

Ezra

1. STATISTICS

Writer is Ezra, great-grandson of Hilkiah, an Aaronic priest-scribe (7:1; II Kings 22:8); time of writing about 450 B.C.; time covered, 93 years; key thought, restoration; key verse, 7:10; type of book, history, Jesephus and Jerome and others have considered Ezra and Nehemiah as one work.

2. THEME

The return of the Jews from captivity in Babylon as led first by Zerubbabel, and second by Ezra constituting, along with Nehemiah, the closing section of Old Testament history. Activities include the restoration of the temple, and the reorganization of national life.

3. OUTLINE

Cyrus' decree (1)   Ezra's expedition (7-10)
Zerubbabel's expedition
   (2-6)

4. SPECIAL CHARACTERISTICS

Important genealogical lists constituted legal records.

Record of two returns: Zerubbabel, 536 B.C.; Ezra, 457 B.C.

This period of restoration is direct result of Daniel 9:1-19.

Between chapters 6 and 7 is a period of 60 silent years. Possibly the events of the book of Esther took place then.

Cyrus fulfilled prophecy spoken 200 years before (Isa. 44:28; 45:1).

Prophecies of Haggai and Zechariah fit into this period.

In world history this was Greece's golden age; the lifetime of Buddha, 563-483; the lifetime of Confucius, 551-479.

The term "Jews" for all the 12 tribes began here (8:35).

5. OUTSTANDING TEACHINGS

In contrast to Assyrian and Babylonian kings, the Persians had a national policy (no doubt God's direction) to repatriate deported people. Thus the way was opened for Israel to return to her land.

The first step in reestablishing the nation was to begin rebuilding the temple and observing national religious feasts. This was wise, and God gave joy in this (chap. 3).

Opposition inevitably developed when God's work began (4:1-22). But with the leadership of the patriots and the encouragement of the prophets, Haggai and Zechariah, the work of the temple was completed.

King Artaxerxes (7:1) was the stepson of Queen Esther. Some 59 years after the dedication of the temple in Jerusalem, Ezra the priest-scribe led another expedition under the King's favorable commandment (7:11-26). Thus Queen Esther may have been responsible under God for the impetus given to the work of the restoration. Ezra took with him 1754 men.

The section of chapters 7-10 shows a period of reform. Ezra found a rather sad situation in Jerusalem. The very thing which God had forbidden was happening without restraint; intermarriage with the peoples of the land. Ezra was astounded.

Ezra's prayer is one of the Bible's great ones (9:5-15). He confessed the sins of the people and they became deeply moved, promising before God to rectify the abuses, especially the unlawful marriages.

The greatest accomplishments of Ezra occurred when God sent another great man to aid him, in the person of Nehemiah. Here are two whose gifts beautifully supplemented each other, supplying to each what the other lacked.

The key to Ezra's character is the statement, "For Ezra had prepared his heart to seek the law of the Lord and do it, and to teach in Israel statutes and judgments" (7:10).

6. INTERESTING FEATURES

From the largest deportation into exile in 606 B.C. to the decree of Cyrus in 536 is just 70 years. From the destruction of the temple (586) to the rebuilding and dedication of the new temple (516) is exactly 70 years.

Jeremiah definitely fixed the period of exile at 70 years in his prophetic words in 25:11 and 29:10.

7. KEY TO UNDERSTANDING

God is behind all that happens to the Jew, opening the

way, encouraging hearts, giving victories. Yet this captivity was but a sample of the world-wide dispersion that was yet to come. Most of the people of God had not learned what God was trying to teach.

Nehemiah

1. STATISTICS

Writer, Nehemiah, cup bearer (i.e., confidant, advisor) to Persian king, Artaxerxes (1:11); possible co-writer, Ezra; time of writing 450 B.C.; years covered, 40; key verse, 2:5, key thought, restoration of defenses of Jerusalem and reforms of the people.

2. THEME

A partially autobiographic history of the completion of the outer and inner defenses of Jerusalem following the captivity, from the pen of a sincere, prayerful man of great faith and courage. Forming a spiritual team with Ezra the priest, Nehemiah governed righteously for God many years.

3. OUTLINE

Prayer (1)
Work on walls (2-6)
Work on internal problems (7-13)

4. SPECIAL CHARACTERISTICS

Nehemiah's expedition (about 444 B.C.) was third at Persian government's expense and with army escort.

Parts of the book are in the first person, possibly taken from the official reports which Nehemiah, as prime minister made to the king.

Nehemiah was a man of great prayer (1:4; 2:4; 4:49; 6:9, 14).

Note that before he made request to the king he spent 4 months in prayer.

5. OUTSTANDING TEACHINGS

God fulfills His purposes. In this case the chosen nation was reestablished by the dictum of heathen kings and by the example of men of faith and courage.

Opposition appeared, as is always the case when a real work for God is being done. Some came as a bulldozing giant, some as a crafty fox. Nehemiah was tested by compromise, ridicule, and by threats of assassination.

Chapter 3 is a commentary on human nature. Among the workers on the wall, some worked "earnestly" (v. 20); some did extra work (vv. 4 and 21); others did not help at all (v. 5); a few did an outstanding job (v. 13). All will meet the record someday.

Building was not the only problem. Evil practices within were equally serious. Nehemiah was able to right this grievous wrong because of his own unselfishness (chap. 5).

As the wall was completed the very next matter was the deepening of the spiritual life. The law of God was read at a public meeting (8:8); then confession was followed by expressions of trust in God and praise. With firm hand Nehemiah corrected abuses of unholy marriages and violating the Sabbath (chap. 13).

6. INTERESTING FEATURES

How to really preach is explained in 8:8.

Some able-bodied daughters helped on the wall (3:12) and even the high priest was not afraid to soil his hands on the wall (3:1).

Prominent in the book are the words "so" and "we."

7. KEY TO UNDERSTANDING

You will understand and enjoy the book more when you put yourself in Nehemiah's place. Against tremendous odds he proved himself to be first a man, then God's man.

Esther

1. STATISTICS

Writer, possibly Mordecai; time of writing about 525 B.C.; events of Esther occur before Nehemiah, possibly between chapters 6 and 7 of Ezra; key thought, God's providential care of His own; key verse, 4:14; purpose, to explain the origin of the Feast of Purim; key characters, Mordecai and Esther.

2. THEME

Even while in exile, because of their sin and God's judgment, still the overruling hand of God covered Israel in protecting, providing care. The eventual purpose of God is not to be frustrated by satanically inspired plots.

3. OUTLINE

Vashti, the queen, deposed: Esther crowned (1, 2)
Haman's plot; Esther's intervention (3-8)
The Jews defend themselves and win (9, 10).

4. SPECIAL CHARACTERISTICS

Name of God is not mentioned but the power of God is clearly seen.

Ahasuerus was King Xerxes of history whose ill-fated expedition against the Greeks in 480 B.C. is well known. The feast in chapter 1 was in preparation for this military venture.

Sushan (Susa), 200 miles east of Babylon, was the winter residence of the Persian kings.

Actually, Esther's marriage made possible the granting of Nehemiah's request and through this, the rebuilding of Jerusalem (Neh. 2:6).

The Feast of Purim (meaning "lot") is still celebrated by the Jewish nation in remembrance of this deliverance from death.

5. OUTSTANDING TEACHINGS

The great truth of God's providence finds here an illustration from history.God maintains a secret control over the affairs of His people, His hidden hand shifts the scenes as necessary. The eye of faith sees the divine factor in all these happenings.

The battle between good and evil is pointed up, with swift judgment for the wicked and overwhelming vindication for the just in the end of the matter.

Grace is beautifully illustrated as Esther voluntarily endangers her life and position for her people.

Satan's smouldering hatred for God and His people find expression in the conflict between Haman and Mordecai.

6. INTERESTING FEATURES

The longest verse in the Bible is 8:9.

Persia seems to have had a well organized postal system (1:22).

Mordecai takes his place along with other talented Jews who were high in governmental position in a foreign land (Daniel and Joseph).

Ahasuerus was known to have an army of over a million men.

7. KEY TO UNDERSTANDING

You will grasp the message of Esther only as you consider the background. Read the last chapters of II Kings and II Chronicles, also books of Ezra and Nehemiah. Through it all remember the unseen hand of God as He directs kings and nations.

Job

1. STATISTICS

Author, actually unknown, possibly Elihu, Moses, or

Job; time, Job lived during patriarchal period; time covered, about 140 years; key thought, one cause of human suffering; key verse, 1:21.

2. THEME

Satan accused God as not being upright in His dealings with man and, to vindicate Himself, He allowed Satan to afflict this well-to-do man of the East to prove the point.

3. OUTLINE

Satan twice challenged Job's prosperity (1, 2)
Three comforters discussed Job's adversity (3-31).
Elihu added new explanation (32-37)
God spoke (38-41)
Job's confession and double restoration (42)

4. SPECIAL CHARACTERISTICS

Job is a dramatic poem with prologue, many scenes, and an epilogue. It is nonetheless completely true.

Possibly the main portion of the book was a public debate with speeches written (13:26). Job was a well known citizen and his tragedy must have occasioned much comment.

No book in Scripture reveals so much of Satan's person and character (i.e., his access to the throne of God.).

Since reference is made to the Flood (14:11) and none to destruction of Sodom and Gomorrah or the giving of the Mosaic law, apparently Job preceded the latter two events.

Job, of all the books of the Bible, contains the greatest concentration of natural theology, works of God in nature.

5. OUTSTANDING TEACHINGS

God is seen to be eminently, minutely aware of the inner character as well as the outward fortunes of one man, Job. He pays priceless compliment to this man's integrity (1:8); on Job's side, his constant practice seemed to be a continual offering of sacrifices to God, both for himself and his family (compare I John 1:7-9).

If God is "buying" the worship of men with gifts of prosperity and health, how can man be a free moral agent? The answer which Job's victory of patience provides is an overwhelming vindication of the honor of God. Job worshiped even under extreme adversity.

A great problem of humanity, the cause of human sufferings, is largely left unanswered. Why? Because the answer is not always possible to give. As Job did, we must leave our case in the hands of God's loving faithfulness.

6. INTERESTING FEATURES

Job is referred to in Ezekiel 14 and James 5.

Job's sickness may have been elephantiasis.

The Lord gave Job twice as much as he had before (42:10).

He lived 140 years after his family and prosperity were restored to him, seeing four generations of descendants.

7. KEY TO UNDERSTANDING

Read the book carefully but do not become lost in the morass of human argument. Keep in view Job's problem—who was to plead his case before God's court? The answer in chapters 31-41 satisfied Job and must satisfy us too.

Psalms

1. STATISTICS

Writers were David (73), Asaph (12), Sons of Korah (12), Solomon (2), Heman (1), Ethan (1), Moses (1), Anonymous (48); time of compostion, over 1000 years from Moses (1500 B.C.) to Ezra (450 B.C.); the title, "Psalm" means a composition set to music; key word, worship; key thought. God is near: key psalm, 23.

2. THEME

This collection of musical poems, divinely inspired and covering the complete range of human emotion and experience, was and is the praise book of Israel and the core of their religious worship. It is the book of the heart as well as the songbook of the redeemed today. Without doubt, it is the most widely known and used book of world's literature.

3. OUTLINE

There are five groups of psalms corresponding somewhat to the five books of the Pentateuch (divisions are approximate):

David's songs (1-41)   Anonymous group (90-106)
Devotional group (42-72)   Psalms written late
Liturgical group (73-89)   (107-150)

Each group closes with a glorious doxology.

4. SPECIAL CHARACTERISTICS

The psalms were written largely with a view to musical accompaniment, especially instrumental. Many instruments were used including the winds, such as the shofar, or ram's horn; stringed, harp; percussion, timbrel and cymbals.

Many were acrostics (initial letter of each succeeding verse was alphabetized) such as 9, 10, 24, 34, 37, 111, 112, 119, 145.

Imprecatory psalms called forth the wrath of God upon the enemies of God and His people. These include: 52, 58, 59, 69, 109, 140.

An important theme is the person and work of Christ. Our Lord suggested this in Luke 24:44.

Psalms are quoted 90 times in the New Testament. They teach morality, history and appreciation of prophecy.

5. OUTSTANDING TEACHINGS

God's omnipotence (107:25-29); His omniscience (147:4,

5); His holiness (99:9); His justice (11:4-7); His mercy (86:15); His faithfulness (119:90).

Israel and Jerusalem are the subject of many psalms showing God's great affection for the city of the great King.

No other book in the Bible so magnifies the Word of God. There is much evidence substantiating the inspiration of the Scriptures.

Many psalms were produced under great crises. Ps. 51 was the occasion of David's great sin; Ps. 18, David's deliverance.

Psa. 22, 23, 24 form a trilogy about the theme of the Shepherd representing the cross, the crook and the crown.

6. INTERESTING FEATURES

The word "Selah" evidently means a musical pause; it is therefore not to be spoken.

Ps. 136 has all of its 26 verses ending with the same words: "for his mercy endureth forever."

The following psalms are prophetic of Christ: 2, 8, 9, 16, 22, 24, 31, 41, 45, 46, 67, 60, 72, 89, 93, 110, 118, 132.

The Septuagint credited Psa. 1 and 119 to Ezra the priest, and that they were the last to be added to the canon of the Psalms.

The psalms of "ascent" were generally sung when pilgrimages were being made to temple feasts.

The last five psalms are called the "hallelujah psalms" as they begin and end with the expression, "Praise ye the Lord."

There are 21 psalms which refer to the history of Israel from the time of the Exodus to the days of restoration.

7. KEY TO UNDERSTANDING

The book of Psalms deals with life—your life. You will find the cause and the cure of every problem in this remarkable book. No matter where else you read in the

Bible, also continue to read the Psalms. The key is to read, study, memorize, love them.

Proverbs

1. STATISTICS

The word "proverb" means a short, pithy, axiomatic saying, particularly appropriate for oral teaching; writers, Solomon (1:1); Agur (30:1), a personal friend of Solomon; King Lemuel (31:1), thought to be another name for Solomon; key thought, value of wisdom; key verse, 9:10; time of writing covers about 300 years (25:1).

2. THEME

Solomon was the wisest man the earth has ever produced (I Kings 3:10). In a day when comparitively few could read and write, the teaching, secular and sacred, was largely by the "proverbial" method, "precept upon precept; line upon line" (Isa. 28:10). Solomon's wisdom was really God's and these sayings profitably fit into life in whatever age they are used.

3. OUTLINE

Wisdom especially for young (1-9)
Various subjects for all (10-24)
Hezekiah's collection (25-29)
Added by Agur and Lemuel (30, 31)

4. SPECIAL CHARACTERISTICS

What Psalms is to the devotional life, Proverbs is to the practical life. Here is concentrated common sense.

In its method of teaching, Proverbs is closely related to the Sermon on the Mount and the epistle of James.

Some proverbs were based on actual experiences, such as 1:7; 4:14.

5. OUTSTANDING TEACHINGS

Underlying emphasis is that true wisdom comes from

fear of (reverence for) the Lord.

The law of God given in the Pentateuch is supported by the admonitions of Proverbs. Wisdom is always God's way.

Many other subjects are dealt with: chastity, proper use of riches, consideration for the poor, control of the tongue, honesty, justice, humanity, cheerfulness, common sense.

6. INTERESTING FEATURES

Perhaps greatest of all proverbs is 3:5, 6. Excellent life verse.

Writer shows real knowledge of nature: ants, spiders, conies.

Respect for parents is a subject most proverbs concerned with.

7. KEY TO UNDERSTANDING

In the structure of Proverbs, God recognizes the ability and limitation of the human mind. Here are mottoes for life, short and easily remembered.

Ecclesiastes

1. STATISTICS

The title "Ecclesiastes" means the Preacher, or the Words of the Preacher; writer, Solomon (1:1); time of writing, about 975 B.C. key verse, 2:11; key thought, emptiness of earthly things; key word, vanity.

2. THEME

Although Solomon was an unusual and gifted king, he allowed sin to have dominion. His marital alliances turned his heart from the sincere worship of God and resulted in emptiness of life and leanness of soul. We have no record of his repentance from such sin, and possibly this monologue was his repentance.

3. OUTLINE

Introduction of writer(1)
Vanity the result of experiment (2, 3)
Vanity the result of observation (3-8)
Mysteries and a conclusion (9-12)

4. SPECIAL CHARACTERISTICS

It is a book of human philosophy on: "Is Life Worth Living?"

Gloomiest outlook of any book in the Bible; no mention of term "Jehovah," a name of God associated with the covenant of redemption.

5. OUTSTANDING TEACHINGS

Although both Job and Ecclesiastes are philosophical treatises on life's problems, the former closes on a happy note while the latter ends on a mournful one. The difference is—no philosophy is complete without God. How exceedingly frightful it is to exclude God's truth about heaven and eternity.

The solution to life's problem is hinted at: there is a divine providence if you will seek it; when you remember God and acknowledge Him, vanity is turned into verity, and vexation into satisfaction. Under the sun there is no profit, but why not look beyond the sun?

6. INTERESTING FEATURES

The "conclusion" (12:13, 14) is still an "under the sun" conclusion.

This book was read at the Jewish Feast of Tabernacles.

Our Lord's commentary on the matter for which Solomon had no answer is found in Luke 12:15.

7. KEY TO UNDERSTANDING

Use the material in Ecclesiastes only after remembering that it is "under the sun" (human, limited) wisdom. Actually the truth in this book should always be supplemented by other (divine truth).

Song of Solomon

1. STATISTICS

Other titles given: "Song of Songs" (Hebrew) meaning the best of Solomon's 1005 songs (I Kings 4:32), "Canticles" meaning song of songs (Latin); writer is undoubtedly Solomon; time of writing, about 1000 B.C.; type of book, dramatic poem; key thought, the delights of married love (spiritual); key phrase, "beloved;" key verse, 6:3.

2. THEME

This is an oriental poem setting forth the tender joys of intimate love. The characters are Solomon and his bride. The spiritual application reveals the love which is between Jehovah and Israel, and between Christ and the Church.

3. OUTLINE

The dialogue suggests dividing at: (1) 1:1—2:6; (2) 2:7—3:5; (3) 3:6—5:1; (4) 5:2—6:9; (5) 6:10—8:4; (6) 8:5—14.

4. SPECIAL CHARACTERISTICS

Like Hebrew poetry, this Song passes suddenly from speaker to speaker and from scene to scene. The identification is usually by the pronouns used. The names of principal characters: Shelomoh (masculine, Prince of Peace) and Shulamith (feminine, Seeker of Peace) correspond, as for example, Julius and Julia; Frank and Frances.

The marriage bond is a favorite figure used by many of the Prophets and the Apostles to represent God's relationship to His people.

5. OUTSTANDING TEACHINGS

The elder daughter in a poor family was apparently charged with the burden and responsibility of much of the labor. She tended the herds and tilled the family vineyard which belonged to King Solomon. One day as she was caring for the flock, she saw a handsome stranger, and they became friends with great affection for each other. One day the stranger departed but promised to return. She believed him, trusted him, and awaited the fulfillment of his promise. Apparently, no one else in the village did. She waited long and dreamed often. And one day he did return, at the head of a glorious procession, and claimed her as his bride.

Another interpretation presupposed what was held by some that the Shulamite was Solomon's bride. Some reasoned that it must have been the daughter of Pharaoh; some the lovely Abishag whom Solomon may have married early in his reign (I Kings 1:3; 2:20-25).

6. INTERESTING FEATURES

The name of God is not mentioned throughout the book.

Shunem was a village on the southwest slope of little Hermon.

This book was always read at the Jews' Passover Feast.

Some regarded the book as a collection of songs to be sung at a marriage feast.

7. KEY TO UNDERSTANDING

A true appreciation of the value of the Song is reserved for those whose hearts are wholly given over to Christ. To them the relationship is quite understandable, and the truths plain.

Isaiah

1. STATISTICS

Writer, Isaiah a prophet living in the reign of Uzziah, Jotham, Ahaz and Hezekiah, kings of Judah (758-694 B.C. Compare 1:1); type of book, judgment-history-prophecy; theme, God's deliverance; key thought, the coming Messiah; key verse, 9:6-7.

2. THEME

Isaiah was the greatest of the writing prophets. With exceptional ability he advised and counseled kings, denounced evil, threatened judgment and added the priceless hope of a better day of peace, blessing and righteousness. His long ministry of 60 years embracing good and bad times, good and bad kings, ended in a violent death under wicked King Manasseh.

3. OUTLINE

Judgment against Judah, Israel and surrounding nations (1-35).

An exceptional page of history showing God's deliverance (36-39).

Looking into near future (Christ's first coming), far future (44-66).

Two main divisions: 39 chapters on judgment; 27 with note of comfort.

4. SPECIAL CHARACTERISTICS

The self dedication that arose from his vision as a youth (6:1) imbued all his writing. Isaiah's style is lofty and rhetorical. He used many vivid figures of speech along with biting sarcasm and ridicule.

As a poet, orator, statesman and prophet he was bold, fearless and thoroughly sincere. Whether before a king or a multitude he did not hesitate to denounce sin or predict judgment.

Contemporaries were: Hosea, Nahum and Micah.

5. OUTSTANDING TEACHINGS

Isaiah's vision and response explain his tremendous accomplishments (6:1-13). Dedicated men of his type are greatly needed in every age.

As a young man he observed his country's high degree of power and prosperity, rivaling the days of Solomon. Prosperity brought on internal greed and worldliness. True worship deteriorated into formality and hypocrisy and God called on His ministers to show the inevitable judgment for sinful conduct.

One of the Old Testament's greatest prophecies is 7:14 where our Lord's virgin birth is foretold.

A passage of more than unusual interest (14:12-17) reveals the nature of Satan's rebellion and its consequence.

Many of Isaiah's prophecies dealt with then current problems. Before him were the threatening ambitions of Assyria and Egypt with the Kingdom of Judah in between. On its borders were the peoples of Syria, Moab, Philistia and Edom. It was concerning the destiny of these nations that he wrote.

One of the most remarkable predictions of the entire Bible was the naming of Cyrus as God's deliverer for His people some 200 years before his birth (41:25; 44:28-45:4).

The climax of the prophet's messianic message is chapter 53.

6. INTERESTING FEATURES

Our Lord quoted 61:1, 2 in the synagogue in Nazareth (Luke 4:20).

A great national prayer of Isaiah is in 63:7-19.

Because of its salvation content, some have called Isaiah the fifth gospel. Hezekiah's most unusual answer to prayer is recorded in chapter 37.

7. KEY TO UNDERSTANDING

You will greatly love the book of Isaiah. Read it with a background of the four gospels. Rejoice also in its foreview of coming blessing and glory.

Jeremiah

1. STATISTICS

Writer, Jeremiah (name means "Jehovah exalted")

priest-prophet to Judah; time of ministry, 626-584 B.C., preceding Babylonian captivity; general theme, warnings of impending judgments; key verse, 1:18; key thought, "go and cry."

2. THEME

Jeremiah, an Aaronic priest, was called to undertake an exceedingly difficult ministry to Judah. He counseled and warned kings (Josiah, Jehoahaz, Jehoiakim, Jehoiachin and Jedekiah) and people of impending judgment, but they only called him a pessimist. He began his ministry about 70 years after the death of Isaiah and lived to see the city destroyed. He was carried captive to Egypt.

3. OUTLINE

Jeremiah's personal history was interwoven among his prophecies.

Josiah's reign (1-12).
Jehoiakim's reign (13-20; 25, 26, 35, 36)
Zedekiah's reign (21-24; 27-34; 37-39)
During Babylonian captivity (40-44)
Concerning the surrounding nations (45-52)

4. SPECIAL CHARACTERISTICS

Written against background of contest between three nations (Assyria, Egypt and Babylonia).

Prophecies are not in chronological order, but written with tenderness and pathos. He has been called the "weeping prophet" due to his intimate concern for the sufferings of the people. Yet in the performance of his God-given ministry, he was fearless, faithful and uncompromising.

Jeremiah was contemporary with Zephaniah, Habakkuk, Daniel and Ezekiel.

5. OUTSTANDING TEACHINGS

At this time there was an abundance of false prophets. These proclaimed peace as Jeremiah announced war;

they foretold prosperity as Jeremiah told of coming trouble. The false prophets were spoken of as patriots, Jeremiah a traitor.

An important prediction regarding Jeconiah (Jehoiachin or Coniah) in 22:28-30 is a strong proof for the virgin birth of Christ, for Joseph the husband of Mary was descended from him (Matt. 1:12, 16).

Jeremiah's writings speak largely of the destiny of surrounding nations of Moab, Ammon, Elam (Persia).

6. INTERESTING FEATURES

Next to Psalms, Jeremiah is the longest book in the Bible. As predicted in chapters 51, 52 Babylon was never rebuilt.

Jeremiah mentions the exact time of the captivity (70 years, 25:9-11.).

7. KEY TO UNDERSTANDING

Jeremiah's sorrow is God's sorrow, Jeremiah's predicted judgment is God's. You can best understand by looking at sin and unrighteousness through God's eyes in whatever age you live.

Lamentations

1. STATISTICS

Writer, Jeremiah; date written, presumably during the three months period between the destruction of Jerusalem and the expedition into Egypt (589 B.C.); key thought, destruction, desolation; key verse, 1:1.

2. THEME

This is a series of funeral hymns composed by the weeping prophet, Jeremiah, following the brutal destruction he had witnessed. He was overcome with grief even though he had been predicting this judgment for many years.

3. OUTLINE

There are 5 chapters or poems. The first 3 are composed of 22 verses as an acrostic; the next has 66 verses or 22 triplets, each triplet with the same initial letter. The last chapter has 22 verses as an acrostic but not in alphabetical form.

4. OUTSTANDING TEACHINGS

This book is mostly remarkable for the great variety of pathetic images it presents, expressing the deepest sorrow. On the other hand, it is rich in expressions of penitence and trust which are offered to God by the afflicted one.

As Jeremiah, stunned and heartbroken viewed the destruction of the city, he understood fully that the judgment had been overwhelmingly justified on God's part (3:22) but he pleaded for a return of God's mercy (3:32, 33).

5. INTERESTING FEATURES

Lamentations is read in Jewish synagogues on the ninth day of the fourth month (July), which is the day of the destruction of the city of Jerusalem (Jer. 52:6, 7).

Following the captivity, Jerusalem was rebuilt and again became a great and powerful city. But the needed lesson was not learned, and in A.D. 70 it was again destroyed.

6. KEY TO UNDERSTANDING

Just as these words are not only Jeremiah's, but God's, so the grief is not only the prophet's, but God's.

Ezekiel

1. STATISTICS

Writer, Ezekiel (means "God will strengthen"), a priest-prophet carried to Babylon by Nebuchadnezzar

(597 B.C.); time of ministry, 26 years (593-567 B.C.); key verses, 3:17-19; key thought, visions and predictions.

2. THEME

Ezekiel was part of the company of captives taken to Babylon, by Nebuchadnezzar in 597 B.C., ten years before the destruction of Jerusalem (II Chron. 36:6, 7). He was placed in a Jewish community by the river Chebar. There he ministered to the exiles who expected momentarily to be allowed to return.His first predictions concerned the destruction of Jerusalem.Following this unhappy event, he consoled and encouraged the captives by predictions of eventual restoration and future blessings. His book is largely taken up with visions, symbolical illustrations, prophecies about surrounding nations and messianic predictions.

3. OUTLINE

Predictions about Jerusalem (1-24)
Predictions about the Gentile nations (25-32, 35)
Predictions about coming restoration (33-48)

4. SPECIAL CHARACTERISTICS

Message directed to the "whole House of Israel" calling attention to the coming restored nation of 12 tribes (12:6, 10; 24:24, 27).

Writing is vigorous and forceful, style vivid and graphic. His visions, object lessons, symbolic actions (mainly the latter) were extremely painful and difficult (i.e., dumbness, lying in one position for a year, eating loathsome food).

The phrase "they shall know that I am God" is found 62 times.

Ezekiel is described as "son of man" 89 times.

5. OUTSTANDING TEACHINGS

Although Ezekiel did not mention Jeremiah, or even his letter to the exiles (Jer. 29), he prophesied ten years concerning the destruction of Jerusalem. Then following the fulfillment, changed to surrounding nations and the coming time of restoration.

As does Isaiah he refers to the fall of Satan in 28:11-19.

Prophecies concerning Tyre were made in detail and have been fulfilled completely in campaigns of Nebuchadnezzar and Alexander the Great.

As a priest, Ezekiel witnessed the desecration and desolation of the temple and looked forward past the temples of Nehemiah and Herod to the marvelous edifice of the millennium.

6. INTERESTING FEATURES

Much of Ezekiel's utterances remain yet to be fulfilled.

The "Plant of Renown" (34:29) evidently refers to the "Branch" (Isa. 11:1).

The sins of Judah (Israel) are thoroughly pictured and denounced as God showed why the exile had to take place.

7. KEY TO UNDERSTANDING

If you keep in mind these three points: Israel's grievous sins; God's inexorable judgment; God's unfailing promises of blessing, you will easily understand Ezekiel's book.

Daniel

1. STATISTICS

Writer, Daniel (name means "God is Judge"), a prince of the Davidic line and a captive from Judea in the first group taken to Babylon by Nebuchadnezzar in 606 B.C. (II Kings 24:14); Daniel lived 90 years, 72 of these as a high government official; key thought, world empires; key verse, 1:20; type of book, personal history—world prophecy; time covered 72 years (4 dynasties).

2. THEME

Because he "purposed in his heart" God exalted him

and as a result of his righteous living he became Prime Minister in Babylon. During this time he received a series of visions depicting the major divisions of world history, particularly as they affect the Jewish nation.

3. OUTLINE

Historical (1-6)   Prophetic (7-12)

4. SPECIAL CHARACTERISTICS

Two languages used: 2:4-7:28 in Aramaic (similar to ancient Chaldee) written for Gentiles and dealing with world history; the rest of the book in Hebrew for Daniel's people and dealing with God's leading and preservation of His own.

First section (1-6), Daniel is spoken of in the third person; in last section (7-12), Daniel himself is narrator.

Daniel was contemporary to leaders at time of exile: Jeremiah, Ezekiel, Joshua (Ezra 3:2), and Zerubbabel.

Daniel undoubtedly knew of the 70-year exile prophesied by Jeremiah (25:12; 29:10).

Three times called "greatly beloved" (9:23; 10:11, 19), Daniel was courageous, consistent, sincere, diligent, a man of great prayer.

5. OUTSTANDING TEACHINGS

The power of steadfast resolution illustrated an introduction to Daniel's character (king's meat and bowing to image refused).

The "lion's den" experience late in Daniel's life (age 70) spoke of his complete confidence in God. It was a rugged test, but how worthwhile (chap. 6).

The testimony of the greatest monarch who ever lived (according to God's estimate in 2:37, 38) ought to be required reading for all rulers, both great and small. (See chap. 4).

While all Daniel's prophecies deal with Gentile world empires, the viewpoint is always, as it were, over the shoulder of Daniel's people, the Jewish nation.

The prophecy of Daniel's 70 weeks (Hebrew, "heptads"

or sevens) anticipated the two comings of Israel's Messiah. The last "seven" refers to the Great Tribulation period still in the future.

6. INTERESTING FEATURES

Daniel, not mentioned by name in Heb. 11, is referred to as one who "stopped the mouths of lions" (v. 33).

Ministry of angels (good and bad) suggested in 8:16; 10:13.

Many Bible scholars believe Belshazzar (5:2, 18) was really the grandson of Nebuchadnezzar, and was co-ruler with his absent father, Nabonidus.

Cyrus the Persian, who conquered Babylon and later released the Jews, was possibly influenced by the statesman, Daniel, reading the prophecies to him.

7. KEY TO UNDERSTANDING

First satisfy your heart with the entire trustworthiness of Daniel in the first six chapters. Then, supply yourself with ample time and dependable study helps for the exacting and thrilling experience of understanding the remainder of his book.

Hosea

1. STATISTICS

Writer, Hosea (name means "salvation"), prophet for more than 60 years to Israel (10 tribes) 790-722 B.C.; key thought, warnings of judgment, key verse, 1:2; type of book, a personal object lesson applied to the sins of the nation.

2. THEME

The Northern Kingdom had enjoyed great temporal prosperity under Jeroboam II, but became increasingly idolatrous and morally corrupt. Hosea was called to denounce sin and warn of inevitable judgment. His experience with his prodigal wife was to be an object lesson to Israel regarding her relationship to God.

3. OUTLINE

Hosea's personal object lesson (1-3)
The message of rebuke, punishment and coming pardon (4-14)

4. SPECIAL CHARACTERISTICS

Hosea's style is concise and abrupt; there are many figures of speech and some intermixed metaphors; but the prophet's sincere sympathy is clearly seen. The writer was described as the "prophet of divine love."

Contemporary with Isaiah (in Judah), Hosea prophesied during the reigns of Uzziah, Jotham, Ahaz and Hezekiah, kings of Judah.

5. OUTSTANDING TEACHINGS

The outward prosperity under Jeroboam II sowed seeds of spiritual anarchy and decay. The princes were murderers, profligates; the priests were deceitful, shameless; the people sank to the lowest level of indecency and idolatry. It was against this condition that Hosea was called to minister.

Through the prophet's own bitter sorrow with his wife's behavior, he was able to comprehend in a measure God's grief over the spiritual adultery of His people.

6. INTERESTING FEATURES

Hosea's children were named for spiritual lessons.

Among his remarkable predictions are those which foretold the downfall of Samaria; the deliverance of Judah; the punishment of Judah; the final restoration of both Israel and Judah.

7. KEY TO UNDERSTANDING

God has the same grief over the spiritual conditions of unfaithful Christians today. The message of Hosea is current and exceedingly pertinent.

Joel

1. STATISTICS

Writer, Joel (name means "Jehovah is God"), probably earliest of the Judean prophets who prophesied in the reigns of Joash and Uzziah (II Chron. 23-26); key thought, judgment and restoration; key verse, 2:13; time, 810-795 B.C., possibly later.

2. THEME

Joel, evidently not a priest, was an inhabitant of Jerusalem in the time of comparative prosperity and was called of God to show similarity of devastating plague of locusts and an accompanying drought, to calamities coming on the nation for its sins. As is frequently the case, Joel looks forward prophetically to the future glorious restoration and subsequent events.

3. SPECIAL CHARACTERISTICS

May have been contemporary with Amos and Hosea in Israel.

The prophet's style is clear and vigorously descriptive.

4. OUTSTANDING TEACHINGS

One of the worst calamities which can come on an agricultural people is a plague of locusts or grasshoppers. Literally, they devour every leaf and blade of green grass in their path. How intensely graphic would be the warning which would promise similar disaster from an enemy invasion.

Joel's greatest prophecy concerns the outpouring of the Holy Spirit, first at Pentecost (2:28, 32; Acts 16:21) and then in greater fulness at the end of the "times of the Gentiles."

Apparently, the prophet emphasized the warring aspect of the times of the end of the age as he calls for plowshares to be turned to swords, and pruning hooks into spears (see reverse, Micah 4:3).

The great assemblage in the valley of Jehoshaphat (3:2 evidently concerns the judgment of the Gentile nations at the end of the Tribulation period (Matt. 25:32).

5. KEY TO UNDERSTANDING

Joel is another of God's great worthies, called upon to add an indispensable part to the great tapestry of truth. The Apostle Peter built his entire message on the day of Pentecost on the prophecy of Joel.

Amos

1. STATISTICS

Writer, Amos, a herdsman-gardener of Tekoa (village south of Bethlehem, 1:1); date of writing 785-750 B.C.; ministered to Israel (Northern Kingdom); key thought, unrighteousness brings judgment; key word, captivity; key verse, 4:12; contemporary of Hosea; prophesied during the reign of Jeroboam II (in Israel) while Uzziah (II Chron. 26) was king in Judah.

2. THEME

This Judean was sent by God to warn Israel of impending judgment if the nation did not repent. During the long prosperity under Jeroboam II and consequent sin, corruption and idolatry, he prophesied judgment and closed his ministry by calling attention to the future restoration and glory of the nation Israel.

3. OUTLINE

There are three divisions: prophecies concerning other nations (1-2); concerning Israel (3:1-9:10); future blessing (9:11-15).

4. SPECIAL CHARACTERISTICS

The prophet's style of writing is simple and reflects his

herdsman background. There is also clarity, directness and practical application. Amos has certain familiarity with the message of Deuteronomy (Compare 2:10 with Deut. 29:5; 4:6-10 with Deut. 28:22).

Amos opens with a statement (1:2) and closes his prophecies with the same exhortation suggesting acquaintance with Joel.

5. OUTSTANDING TEACHINGS

Amos strongly suggests the inevitability of judgment for the sins of surrounding nations, but that the God who must punish sin there, must also punish sin in Israel. The logic is inescapable.

The book follows the general prophetical pattern; with warnings of coming judgment, then with promises of eventual blessing.

6. INTERESTING FEATURES

Amos is quoted in the New Testament by Stephen in Acts 7:42, 43 and by James in Acts 15:15-17.

7. KEY TO UNDERSTANDING

Though Israel was outstandingly wicked, God was gracious and patient. He is still the same today.

Obadiah

1. STATISTICS

Writer, Obadiah (background unknown); name means "Servant of Jehovah;" time of writing, 586-583 B.C.; key verse, 21; prophesied to Judah; was contemporary with Jeremiah.

2. THEME

The Edomites, descendants of Esau, were bitter enemies of Israel. When Judah was captured and Jerusalem destroyed by Nebuchadnezzar (586 B.C.), the Edomites sided with the conquerors and assisted them hoping to receive a portion of the desolated land for themselves. Concerning this, God inspired Obadiah to prophesy against Edom telling them that their time was coming, "there shall not be any remaining" of that nation.

3. SPECIAL CHARACTERISTICS

There are no references from Obadiah in the New Testament.

More than 20 predictions are given in the Old Testament regarding Edom.Most in Obadiah, but also Isa. 34, 63; Jer. 49 and Ezek. 35.

4. OUTSTANDING TEACHING

The right to judge Israel God reserves for Himself. Other nations (such as Edom) He will severely judge. Indications are in Mal. 1:3-5 that He had done so by 400 B.C.

Present ruins of Edom are impressive. No less than 300 cities are in desolate ruins today, including Petra or Sela.Nothing more is known of Edom following A.D. 70.

Edom was not to rise again, but for Israel there is promise of future glory.

5. INTERESTING FEATURES

Obadiah is the shortest book in the Old Testament.

King Herod, the one responsible for the slaughter of innocent babies in Matt. 2:16-18, was an Edomite (Idumean).

6. KEY TO UNDERSTANDING

It is imperative that we view Obadiah's utterances from the standpoint of God's over-all purpose. Edom became illustrative of any nation that failed to recognize God's eventual purpose for His chosen people.

Jonah

1. STATISTICS

Writer, Jonah (II Kings 14:25), one of the earliest of

writing prophets; time of writing, 785-767 B.C., during reign of Jeroboam II; Jonah's home in Gath-Hepher in Northern Kingdom; key word, Nineveh (capital of Assyria); key verse, 3:2; time, soon after Elisha.

2. THEME

Assyria, a rising world power, was idolatrously wicked before God. Jonah, a prophet of Israel, was commissioned to offer Nineveh God's ultimatum. However Jonah, willing that Nineveh should be destroyed so the threat to the well-being of Israel might be removed, took ship in the opposite direction. God changed his direction and Jonah went to Nineveh, and his preaching brought complete repentance.

3. SPECIAL CHARACTERISTICS

Jonah was the only prophet in the Bible who endeavored to conceal his message.

Here is a prophet of Israel, called of God to prolong the life of a Gentile nation.

Except for the miracle of the fish experience, the people of Nineveh would have paid little attention to Jonah.

The book closes with a beautiful lesson on God's care and compassion for little children (4:11).

4. OUTSTANDING TEACHINGS

There is no problem with the "fish" part of the story when we understand that God "prepared" it (1:17); God prepared other things also (4:6-8).

The heart of the story revealed that Nineveh's sins and impending destruction became a giant object lesson to Israel who was committing the same sins.

Another lesson: God desired to show His compassion for other nations so that Israel would understand the gospel of Christ ought to be preached to all nations.

Jonah's story is proof of the foolishness of trying to escape from God. He has thousands of ways at His command to bring about willing obedience.

5. INTERESTING FEATURES

The word "whale" is better translated "sea monster" or "fish."

Tarshish possibly refers to Tartessus, a city in Spain.

Nineveh was a huge city, thought to be 60 to 90 miles in circumference, with walls enclosing gardens and pastures.

6. KEY TO UNDERSTANDING

There is absolutely no difficulty in accepting and understanding the narrative of the book if your concept of God is large enough. Surely, a God who could make a world could also "prepare" a fish to bring about the completion of His will.

Micah

1. STATISTICS

Writer, Micah (full name Micaiah) meaning "Who is like Jehovah?"; a prophet from Moresh-Gath (30 miles S.W. of Jerusalem) who ministered to both Judah and Israel; time of prophecy, 751-693 B.C. in the reigns of Jotham, Ahaz and Hezekiah and before the fall of Samaria (722 B.C.). He was a contemporary of Isaiah and Hosea; key thought, controversy; key verse, 6:2.

2. THEME

Little is said of his personal history, the book is given over to reproof and warning to both Kingdoms. Micah has been called the "prophet of social reform" due to his emphasis on the sins of the rulers and false religious leaders against the people. National shortcomings are also emphasized with judgment promised. There is a better day coming for God's people.

3. SPECIAL CHARACTERISTICS

Though Assyria was world dominant, Micah's prophecy was concerning Babylon's conquest (4:10) which was not to take place for another century.

Micah's style is poetically beautiful and vigorous. He is quite clear in his predictions of coming punishment although there are passages that are somewhat obscure.

Much of the subject matter concerns the capitals, Jerusalem and Samaria. As to the latter, it was to become "as an heap of the field" (1:6); Jerusalem was to become "heaps" (3:12).

4. OUTSTANDING TEACHINGS

It was to Micah's prophecy the scribes of Jerusalem referred when the wicked King Herod sought to know concerning the birth of the new King (Matt. 2:2-6; Mic. 5:2).

A glorious passage (somewhat identical with Isa. 2:2-4) is found in 4:1-5 as the prophet speaks of a warless, prosperous, Godly world with God's chosen people in the foreground.

Other prophetic subjects include the invasion by Shalmaneser (1:6-8); invasion by Sennacherib (1:9-16); the dispersion of Israel (5:7, 8); the cessation of prophecy (3:6, 7); the utter destruction of Jerusalem (3:12).

5. INTERESTING FEATURES

Jeremiah refers to Micah in his prophecy (Jer. 26:18, 19).

Some say the greatest verse in the Old Testament is 6:8.

One of the Old Testament's major Messianic predictions is in Micah 5:2.

6. KEY TO UNDERSTANDING

God uses men to proclaim His message. Here, through the instrumentality of a chosen man, some amazing details of future history are given to all who will hear. As always, God warns before He sends punishment.

Nahum

1. STATISTICS

Writer, Nahum, a prophet of Elkosh (possibly related to

later Capernaum which means "village of Nahum") in Galilee whose name means "consolation;" time of writing, approximately 100 years after Jonah (663-633 B.C.); key word, doom; key verses 1:8, 9.

2. THEME

Essentially, Nahum is a continuation of Jonah with the latter recording the repentance of Nineveh, and Nahum its predicted doom. Humanly speaking, Nahum's prediction was impossible as Nineveh was the impregnable capital of a world-ruling empire. But as predicted, the vast Assyrian nation came to certain doom about 100 years after Nahum prophesied. The book of Nahum is almost wholly taken up with this one theme.

3. SPECIAL CHARACTERISTICS

Assyria's policy concerning captive peoples was one of exceeding cruelty. Its enormous wealth was gained mostly by plundering surrounding nations. Nahum likened it to a den of lions (2:1-13) which became beasts of prey. Captives were mutilated by having eyes torn out and tongues extracted.

Nahum's prediction brought comfort to hearts of dwellers in Jerusalem, for Assyria had been the hated and feared enemy for nearly two centuries.

4. OUTSTANDING TEACHINGS

While God's people had sinned, and God in faithfulness had to punish them, still the nations which He used came to know His wrath also, and this was the case with the Assyrian Empire.

The collapse of Nineveh and the Assyrian Empire came suddenly. The Medes and Babylonians had besieged the capital for two years when a sudden flood of the Tigris river carried away part of the protecting wall and opened the way for the attacking army to enter and conquer. This was pre-written by Nahum 100 years before.

There is a possible reference to the disastrous defeat of Sennacherib as he confronted Jerusalem (II Kings 19:35), in 1:10-13. The untimely end of the king himself is outlined in the following verses.

5. INTERESTING FEATURES

Ezekiel (31:3-14) and Zephaniah (2:13-15) besides Jonah concern themselves with Nineveh's fate.

The city's walls were 100 feet high and broad enough to drive four spans of chariot horses abreast; there were 1500 watch towers, for defenses. There was never a prophecy more unlikely!

6. KEY TO UNDERSTANDING

Who but God could predict minutely events of such magnitude and infinitude hundreds of years before they came to pass? This is true comfort to those who study prophecy today relating to tomorrow. God is faithful.

Habakkuk

1. STATISTICS

Writer, Habakkuk, a little known prophet (name means "embrace") who ministered in the reigns of Josiah and Jehoiakim, possible 612-598 B.C.; key verse, 2:4; key thought, faith in God. Habakkuk was a contemporary of Jeremiah and prophesied in Judah.

2. THEME

To the prophet was given the vision of the coming captivity of God's people by Babylonians. Already Nebuchadnezzar had carried off some nobles (including Daniel in 606 B.C.) and there were two other deportations to follow (597 and 586 B.C.). Habakkuk's sensitive heart was torn by the devastation of his land. God answered by setting forth the coming doom of the Babylonians and the book ends with the prophet's prayer of complete confidence in God.

3. SPECIAL CHARACTERISTICS

There is almost a dialogue between God and Habakkuk,

as the prophet inquiringly complains of the problems of good and evil. God patiently answers in chapter 2.

The predictions concerning the fall of Babylon were fulfilled about 70 years later.

Habakkuk has many well quoted passages in the New Testament: particularly 2:4; but also 2:14; 2:20; 3:2; and 3:17, 18.

This book is a very beautiful example of poetic prophecy.

Chapter 3 was evidently a psalm to be used in public worship.

4. OUTSTANDING TEACHINGS

The prophet was desperately concerned with the evil in his own land. So to him God revealed the coming invasion of the enemy, Babylon, to punish the nation for its sins. Habakkuk answered by asking God why Israel should be punished for sin by a nation more sinful than itself. God's answer was that the "just" would still live by faith, and that He would also punish Babylon in due time. The prophet was satisfied and prayed for speedy deliverance of the people.

5. KEY TO UNDERSTANDING

The great standard by which Israel and all the nations of the world will be judged is the holiness and righteousness of God.

Zephaniah

1. STATISTICS

Writer, Zephaniah, prophet to Judah was a great-great-grandson of one Hizkiah, believed by many to be King Hezekiah. He would thus be of royal lineage. Little is known of this prophet whose name means "Jehovah has guarded." His ministry (638-608 B.C.) was in the reign of King Josiah which makes him the first of the Chaldean prophetic messengers. Key thought, the coming day of

God's wrath; key verse, 1:14-16.

2. THEME

The Kingdom of Judah apparently was to have profited from the experience of Israel's captivity, for God sent no prophet to them during the reign of wicked King Manasseh until Zephaniah. The revival under Josiah soon degenerated with the idea of tolerance allowing anyone to choose his own religion. This, God could not allow, and Zephaniah was sent to call attention to certain judgment unless complete repentance followed.

3. OUTLINE

Way of wrath for Judah (1)

Day of wrath for the nations (2)

Day of wrath for Jerusalem with coming blessing (3)

4. SPECIAL CHARACTERISTICS

Zephaniah's prophecy was the most comprehensive of all prophetic utterances, spoken as it were, to all nations under heaven.

The phrase "great day of the Lord," or similar words, is emphasized in 1:7 and repeated nine times through chapters 1-3.

5. OUTSTANDING TEACHINGS

Above all other prophets, Zephaniah sees the entire earth as the theater of God's universal government. From every quarter nations are chosen as examples of His judgment (2:4-15), but Judah failed to learn the lesson.

The prophecy regarding the four cities of Philistia shows that prophecy and providence are guided by the same hand.

6. KEY TO UNDERSTANDING

It is true that God is love. But this is not the entire description of the character of God. He is also wrath against all ungodliness, wherever it is found.

Haggai

1. STATISTICS

Writer, Haggai, one of three post-exilic prophets; time of ministry, following the 70-year exile in Babylon; key verses, 2:6-9; key word, build; time, 520-518 B.C.

2. THEME

Haggai returned with the first expedition led by Zerubbabel, along with Ezra the scribe (Ezra 3:8; Hag. 1:1). Work began on the restoration of the temple, only to run into opposition from former inhabitants of the land. God inspired the prophet, who urged the work forward.

3. SPECIAL CHARACTERISTICS

Four messages of Haggai were spoken within a period of only four months.

It is possible that Haggai may have personally seen the glory of the temple of Solomon (2:3). This would have made him a very old man at the time of his prophetic ministry.

The messages are exceedingly condensed and perhaps were a summary of that which was given orally.

Each time Haggai's name is mentioned, he is called "the prophet" thus emphasizing his important ministry.

4. OUTSTANDING TEACHINGS

Opposition to the work caused the people to leave it and turn to more profitable pursuits. They rationalized that the time had not come for rebuilding. Adorning their homes, propagating their flocks and working their fields occupied their interests. Haggai's impassioned plea roused them again to action.

Haggai's first message was in substance that of Matthew 6:33. In the second he stressed that the glory of the new temple would be greater than the first. He told them that certain plagues had come on them due to their neglect of the important task, and the last message was specially to Zerubbabel promising him that God would destroy the enemy and that His people would endure and prosper.

5. KEY TO UNDERSTANDING

God will not be frustrated nor change in His purposes; He uses men to fulfill His plans.

Zechariah

1. STATISTICS

Writer, Zechariah (1:1) whose name means "God is Renown," was of the priestly tribe, possibly born in Babylon. He returned with the first expedition; called to encourage the builders with a view of the glorious future; time, 520-518 B.C.; key thought, God is in this work; key verse, 14:9.

2. THEME

The first returning group of exiles was 50,000 strong, but had been hindered and finally stopped building. God spoke through Zechariah (and Haggai) to stir up their hearts and renew their labors. While Haggai's burden seemed to be the religious life of the people, Zechariah's was to concentrate on the national and political. His ministry extended over two years and he was used to bring to completion the restoration of the temple. His main ministry looked far into the future envisioning both the first coming of the Messiah and His return in power and great glory.

3. SPECIAL CHARACTERISTICS

Book is divided: eight visions (given in a single night) dealing with a large variety of subjects (1-6); four given directly to a questioning company from Babylon (7:2, 3) answering their problems; two burdens (chaps. 7 and 8) concerning future oppression and eventual triumph (9-14.

The expression "Thus saith the Lord" is found 89 times; the term "The Lord of hosts" 36 times.

Zechariah contains more specific promises relative to the crucifixion than any other Old Testament book except Psalms (9:9; 11:12, 13; 13:6, 7).

4. OUTSTANDING TEACHINGS

In spite of meager circumstances and coming opposition for the chosen people, God is still to triumph and with Him, His people.

A detail to remember is the intermingling of the work of the Messiah, first as suffering Saviour, then as resistless Sovereign.

God's watchful interest in other nations is clearly demonstrated both in relation to their sin and idolatry, and with reference to their treatment of Israel.

A delightful picture of the future is presented in the coming happiness of Zion with streets full of children (8:3-5) and all nations of the world coming to the Jews to learn of their God (8:22, 23).

5. KEY TO UNDERSTANDING

Life is not concerned with time alone. There is an overruling power which works in time to prepare for eternity. The Jewish nation is but an example of the great passion of the heart of God for the sons of men.

Malachi

1. STATISTICS

Writer, Malachi (name means "My Messenger") was a contemporary of Nehemiah; he prophesied against the same abuses Nehemiah described; time, 435-425 B.C.; key word, a curse; key thought, the love of God in spite of the sins of His people; key verses, 3:16, 17. Though linked with Haggai and Zechariah as a post-exilic prophet, he ministered about 100 years later.

2. THEME

Malachi's prophecy was interwoven with Nehemiah's history. Both labored to rebuild moral life of the people as well as the walls of Jerusalem. When Nehemiah returned to Babylon for a period of time Malachi ministered to the people concerning their sins and moral abuses. He looked beyond to the coming day of the Lord.

3. OUTLINE

Carelessness in things of God (1:1-14)
Sinful lives of the priests (2:1-9)
Widespread unfaithfulness to God, to others (2:10-16)
Bitter complaint against God's dealings (2:17; 3:13-15).

4. SPECIAL CHARACTERISTICS

The great prophecy of John the Baptist is in 3:1-30, and he actually is the only prophet who is himself the subject of prophecy.

The sin of offering "diseased animals" to the Lord is soundly condemned in 1:8-10. It is treated as an insult to God.

The last word in the Old Testament is "curse." It remains for the New Testament to bring blessing.

5. OUTSTANDING TEACHINGS

Malachi predicts the coming of Elijah (4:5), partially fulfilled in John the Baptist (Matt. 11:14). Since he did not usher in the "great and terrible day of the Lord" at that time the prediction has a second fulfillment in the future. Possibly, he may be one of the two witnesses in Revelation 11.

The matter of withholding tithes and offerings is treated as robbery (3:8-15). The Mosaic Law pronounced the tithe as "belonging" to the Lord. Here the people were selfishly using it for other things.

The essential message of Malachi is an epitome of the entire Old Testament. God rebukes corruption and promises deliverance and blessing on obedience. The viewpoint is that of the authority of the present law, but also of the riches of grace which God has in store for the age of blessing.

6. KEY TO UNDERSTANDING

Take a broad look at Malachi. It is the same old story of sin and unrighteousness. Mankind has not changed in all these years. But turn around and look the other way. There is coming a day of light when the Sun of Righteousness will arise. Thank God there is also a New Testament!

Between Old and New

• The Old Testament closes with the book of the prophet Malachi, who wrote about the year 400 B.C. While many of the Jews still remained scattered as colonists among the various provinces of the vast Persian Empire, a small nucleus had returned under Ezra and Nehemiah. These Jews had resettled Judea and Jerusalem and had re-established worship of the true God.

• The 400 years between the Old and New Testaments are sometimes called the "silent years" for there is no sacred record given. But from secular history and the Apocrypha we learn that this was a period of unusually great and important activity.

• There was first the persian period. The Old Testament had closed with Judea being a Persian province. Persia had been a world power for 100 years. The Persian rulers were tolerant and the Jews under them enjoyed considerable liberty. This domination continued over Judea for another 100 years with little or no recorded Jewish history.

• Up to this time in history the powers of the world had been found in Asia and Africa. Now came the rising power of Greece under Phillip of Macedon and his son, Alexander the Great.

• Greece is supposed to have come into being around 1000 B.C. or about the time of David and Solomon. At any rate, in 336 B.C., Alexander assumed command of the invincible Grecian army and proceeded to sweep the world, including the Holy Land. Alexander showed great consideration for the Jews and spared the holy city, Jerusalem. But he did establish Greek cities and communities all along his route and along with them Greek culture and Greek language.

• On his death in 323 B.C. the entire empire was divided among his four Generals. Syria was given to Seleucus and Egypt to Ptolemy. The land of Palestine lying between these two first went to Syria and later to Egypt, remaining under Egyptian control for another 100 years.

• Under the reign of the king of Egypt called the "Ptolemies" the conditions of the Jews were peaceful and happy. They emigrated into many places, built synagogues and carried Jewish culture into remote places. It was at this time that Alexandria became an influential center of Judaism.Also at this time, the Septuagint, a translation of the Old Testament into the Greek language was made. All of this peace, however, was soon to end.

• In 198 B.C. Antiochus the Greek king of Syria, reconquered Palestine. At this time the familiar divisions of Galilee, Judea, Samaria, Trachonitis, and Perea were made. The Jews were permitted to live under their own laws, being governed by a high priest and a council.

• About 175 B.C. Antiochus Epiphanes, a cruel and bloody conqueror, appeared. He seems to have utterly despised the Jews and made furious and determined efforts to exterminate them and their religion. He devastated Jerusalem, defiled the temple, forbade circumcision, sold thousands of Jews into slavery, destroyed all copies of the Scripture he could find, and resorted to every conceivable means of torture and death in order to force Jews to renounce their beliefs. This led to the revolt of the Maccabees, one of the most heroic pages in Jewish history.

• Mattathias, the first of the Maccabees (meaning hammer) was a priest of great sanctity and courage. He had five sons of great courage and ability. He organized the revolt. On Mattathias's death, the leadership fell to his son Judas. He won battle after battle against unbelievable and impossible odds. He seemed to possess amazing military genius. He reconquered Jerusalem; purified and rededicated the temple in 165 B.C. This is commemorated in what is since known as the "Feast of the Dedication." He united the military and priestly functions in himself and established a line of "priest-rulers" who governed the land for the next 100 years.

• In the year 63 B.C. the Roman general Pompey conquered the land and Antipater (an Idumean or Edomite) was appointed ruler of Judea. He was succeeded by his son Herod the Great who was king from 37 to 3 B.C. (Most scholars hold to date of 5 or 4 B.C. for the birth of Christ) This is the same Herod who slew all the children in Bethlehem at the time of the birth of Jesus Christ. He was a brutal and cruel man and it was he who built the temple as a favor to the Jews.

• During this long period there appeared many Jewish writings such as the Mishna, the Gemara, the Halochoth, Midrashim, Kabbala. This mass of tradition became so superimposed on the law of God that obedience was transferred from the law to the traditional interpretation.

• So, among such a people, governed under the suzerainty of Rome by an Idumean Usurper, rent by bitter and unspiritual religious controversies, and maintaining elaborate religious ritual, appeared Jesus Christ the Son of God and the King of Israel.

NEW TESTAMENT

Matthew

1. BACKGROUND

Writer, Matthew (also called Levi) a publican or tax collector. Undoubtedly a sagacious man, accustomed to writing, and a student of human nature. His home was Capernaum; he was well versed in the history, poetry, doctrine, prophecy of the Jews. He presents the material in plain, direct language and in an orderly way.

Date of writing is presumedly A.D. 60, approximately 30 years after Christ's death.

He writes of Christ the King; his special readers, the Jews.

2. THEME

The key verse is 1:1. Here is found the subject and purpose. Jesus of Nazareth is the promised King, the Son of David first, and the Son of Abraham (sacrifice) second.

The Messiahship (Kingship) of Christ is emphasized. Christ is the full embodiment of everything the Old Testament Scriptures promised would come. However, He is rejected, and turns to the fulfillment of the sacrificial type (Son of Abraham) at the cross.

3. MAIN DIVISIONS

The King presents Himself to Israel (1-12); the King

rejected, goes to the cross as the sacrificial Son; resurrection and ascension follow (13-28).

4. OUTLINE

Miraculous Birth of the King	Promised Church of the King
Divine Preservation of the King	Glorious Transfiguration of the King
Baptism of the King by John	Searching Discourses of the King
Temptation of the King by the Devil	Triumphal Entry of the King
Remarkable Proclamation of the King	God-Given Wisdom of the King
Wonderful Miracles of the King	Dreadful Denunciations of the King
Preparatory Commission of the King	Second Coming of the Great King
Deliberate Rejection of the King	Foretold Betrayal of the King
Kingdom Parables of the King	Sacrificial Death of the King
Unchanging Compassion of the King	Victorious Resurrection of the King

5. SPECIAL CHARACTERISTICS

Matthew is the "swinging door" or the "hinge book" between the Old and the New Testaments.

There are more than 60 Old Testament references and about 40 quotations from the Old Testament in Matthew.

A characteristic phrase is "that it might be fulfilled."

Matthew presents a genealogical table tracing the Messianic line back to King David.

Two of Christ's major discourses are found here: the Sermon on the Mount, 5; 6; 7; and the Olivet Discourse, 24;25.

An unusual picture of the happenings of this present age is seen prophetically in chapter 13, where 7 parables form one picture.

6. OUTSTANDING TEACHINGS

The Sermon on the Mount applies: (1) to Christ's day; (2) to our day; (3) to the day of the coming Kingdom.

Note the attributes of the King: His Person, Preparation, Propaganda, Program, Passion, Power.

The account of the death and resurrection of Christ takes about 25 percent of the total material in Matthew.

7. KEY TO UNDERSTANDING

Christ is King. He was rejected, crucified, resurrected, but He is still a King and will someday prove this.

Matthew is easy to read. Its material is alive and graphic. Note the "time words." Connect Matthew to the future happenings too.

Mark

1. BACKGROUND

Writer, John Mark (Mark is Roman name), son of one of the New Testament Marys (Acts 12:12) and nephew of Barnabas (13:5). Mark is thought to be an intimate companion of Peter who calls him his son (I Pet. 5:13). Possibly this is largely Peter's gospel but written down by Mark. Also, Mark was the companion of Paul and Barnabas on their first missionary journey. Later he was rejected (Acts 15:37-39) but at the end of Paul's life was much desired (II Tim. 4:11).

Date of the writing is about A.D. 60; written especially to the Romans; Mark presents Christ as Servant (God's).

2. THEME

Mark presents Christ as a mighty Man of Action. He is seen as the Servant of Jehovah. The key word is "power." The key verse is 10:45. The book is filled with deeds. Miracles are much more prominent than discourses. A characteristic word is "straightway" or "immediately" (used 19 and 17 times respectively).

No genealogy is given, for who is interested in the background of a servant? The immediate audience is the Roman who would greatly appreciate such a man of active power.

3. MAIN DIVISIONS

Wonderful works (1-9); wonderful teachings (10-14); wonderful sacrifice (15; 16).

4. OUTLINE

The Manifestation of the Servant-Son (1:1-11)
The Servant-Son Tested as to His Fidelity (1:12, 23)
The Servant-Son at Work (1:14-13:37)
The Servant-Son Obedient unto Death (14:1-15:47)
The Servant-Son now Risen and Given all Authority (16:1-20)

5. SPECIAL CHARACTERISTICS

That the Gospel was written in Rome and for the Romans is strongly evidenced by the frequent use of Latin terms such as "legion" and "centurion." Mark also uses the Roman terms for division of night.

No genealogy is given, for the Romans looked not for a Messiah. Nor is Jewish law mentioned, nor Jewish prophecies.

Mark explains that the Jordan is a river (1:5); and that the Pharisees "used to fast" (2:18); and that the Mount of Olives is "over against the temple" (13:3) for the benefit of those unacquainted with these terms.

Mark has room to mention 20 miracles but only 4 parables. Also, at the crucifixion he quotes the Roman centurion as remarking, "Truly this Man was the Son of God."

6. OUTSTANDING TEACHINGS

Mark deals somewhat (1:24; 1:32-34; 3:11, 12) with the problem of demon possession. Are demons real? Or, is this just another term for mental affliction?

The rather plain teaching of Scripture is that the

demon-possessed were not merely lunatic but were cases of "invaded personality."

Christ's casting out of demons therefore was definite and real, and a mark of His power over the massed forces of evil.

The miracles in Mark are very prominent. They include 17 bodily cures, 9 miracles over the forces of nature, 6 cures of demoniacs, 3 raised from the dead. In addition, Jesus accomplished uncounted other (1:32-34; 6:53-56) miracles.

These manifestations of divine power are a mark of God's authentication of Jesus' mission (see John 15:24).

7. KEY TO UNDERSTANDING

Look for "plenty of action" in Mark's Gospel. Christ is a Man of power. He has everything at His fingertips. As such, He appeals to men of action in all centuries, particularly young men, men of industry and business, men of science. To these, Christ can easily become their Ideal.

Luke

1. BACKGROUND

Writer, Luke, a physician, possibly a Greek, and an intimate companion of the Apostle Paul in many of his journeys. Luke is not one of the disciples, but evidently knew them all personally, and derived much of his knowledge of Christ directly from their lips (1:1-3).

This Gospel account is dedicated to an important Greek nobleman named Theophilus (as is Acts also).

The time of writing is about A.D. 60, possibly while the Apostle Paul was in prison in Caesarea.

The content of the book presents Christ as Son of Man; the book is particularly addressed to the Greeks.

2. THEME

Luke presents Christ as the ideally perfect Man with all

the beauty and perfection of His spotless humanity. Christ is seen with all the strength of manhood, yet gentle, with supreme knowledge, with commanding willpower, with conscientious faithfulness, and with devotion to His Father's will even unto death. The key verse is 19:10. The key thought is the Son of Man among men.

The appeal is to the cultured, educated of earth. Christ is shown to be highest Ideal of all humanity.

3. MAIN DIVISIONS

Introduction (1:14); human relationships of Jesus (1:5-2:52); baptism, ancestry, and testing of Jesus (3:1-4:13); Christ's ministry as Prophet-King in Galilee (4:14-9:50); from Galilee to Jerusalem (9:51-19:44); final offer as King, rejection, sacrifice (19:45-23:56); resurrection, resurrection ministry, and ascension (24:1-53).

4. OUTLINE

Preparation
John the Baptist (1)
Birth and Infancy (2)
Baptism and Temptation (3)
Temptation (4)
Preaching
Disciples Chosen (5)
Healing Miracles (5)
Sermon on Mount (6)
Miracles (7)
Demoniac (8)
Disciples Commissioned (9)

Feeding 5,000 (9)
Samaritan Ministry (9-18)
Passion
Predictions (9:22, 44)
Transfiguration (9)
Publicans and Pounds (19)
Triumphal Entry (19)
Enemies Exposed (20)
Second Coming Described (21)
Last Night (22)
Crucifixion (23)
Resurrection (24

5. SPECIAL CHARACTERISTICS

This Gospel is the longest and most comprehensive of all four. The writer presents many things not given by Matthew or Mark. He is meticulous about detail, especially chronological. Many times we can see Luke's medical knowledge showing through. He notes that Simon's mother-in-law had a "great" fever (4:38); and the man's "withered" hand was his "right" hand (6:6); and that the daughter of Jairus was "12 years" of age.

When he gives the genealogy of Christ he takes the line clear back to Adam, for this is the table of ancestry of the perfect Man.

The humanity of Christ is especially manifested as He weeps over Jerusalem (19); as He touches the ear of the injured Malchus (22); and as He tenderly comforts the dying thief (23).

The foundation passage for 5 of the great songs of the Church is in chapters 1 and 2.

6. OUTSTANDING TEACHINGS

The intimate story of the virgin birth as given in Luke is truly magnificent. A delicate subject is handled with frankness, beauty, and restraint.

Christ is Master of the spoken word here. He speaks with truth, power and authority.

7. KEY TO UNDERSTANDING

Expect to find here not only the greatest Man, Teacher, Example, Ideal, but also the pre-existent, virgin born, God of Eternity. You will not be disappointed.

John

1. BACKGROUND

Writer, John, brother of James, son of Zebedee, former fisherman and writer of 4 other New Testament books.

The time of writing is late, about A.D. 95. John was about 95 too.

Perhaps the most widely circulated piece of literature in world, because of practice of printing and distributing John's Gospel by itself.

2. THEME

God has called on John to present the **spiritual** portrait of Christ. Jesus Christ is the true Son of God, come for a time to be clothed in human flesh. But nonetheless the pre-existent eternal second Person of the blessed Trinity. In no other piece of literature is the deity of Christ more persistently affirmed or definitely proved.

The key verse and thought is found in 20:30, 31.

All the elements in John, the prologues, the miracles, the discourses, the prophetic utterances, the unique death, resurrection and ascension . . . all blend in one grand declaration . . . Christ is God.

3. MAIN DIVISIONS

The Word is Christ (1:1-14); witness of John the Baptist (1:15-34); public ministry of Christ (1:35-12:50); private ministry of Christ (13:1-17:26); sacrifice of Christ (18:1-19:42); Christian resurrection (20:1-31); epilogue: Christ, Master of service (21:1-25).

4. OUTLINE

Word Made Flesh (1)	Good Shepherd (10)
Marriage at Cana (2)	Lazarus Raised (11)
Nicodemus (3)	Mary's Gift (12)
Woman at Well (4)	Washing Feet (13)
Man at Pool (5)	Farewell (14-16)
5,000 Fed (6)	Prayer (17)
At the Feast (7)	Crucifixion (18, 19)
Sinful Woman (8)	Alive Again (20, 21)
Blind Man (9)	

5. SPECIAL CHARACTERISTICS

The material in John is unique. John writes of events, discourses, and miracles not mentioned by the other three writers. So the material is beautifully supplemental and positively essential.

The great premise of the Gospel is that the deity of Christ is an absolute essential to salvation. Only the eternal Son of the eternal God could possibly save us.

To carry out the purpose of the Gospel, John relates these miracles, among "many other signs," to prove His deity; all attest Christ's supernatural character. For instance, the water was changed into wine **without a word;** the nobleman's son is healed **at a distance;** the man healed had been crippled **for 38 years;** Lazarus was raised after he had been dead **for four days;** the blind man had not seen **from birth.**

John emphasizes that the atonement was the great purpose of Christ's coming. Most of John's narrative centers about the religious feasts Christ attended at Jerusalem. John records Jesus' participation in five feasts: 2; 3-4:3; 5:1-47; 7:2-10:21; 10:22-40; 12:1-20:31.

Perhaps the high spot of John's Gospel is the upper room discourse, found in chapters 13-17. This highly concentrated body of truth has been said to contain all the elements of truth later amplified in the Epistles. The holy of holies here is chapter 17, the intimate prayer between God the Father and God the Son.

6. KEY TO UNDERSTANDING

This all-transcendent writing is the very mountain peak of Bible teachings. Here we find the entrance to the heart of God . . . BELIEVE in His Son. In no portion of the Bible will your heart be lifted higher than in these 21 chapters which show Christ as the God of heaven, being made flesh in order to die for the sons of men.

Acts

1. BACKGROUND

Writer, Luke (same as third Gospel), physician, companion of the Apostle Paul (see Col. 4:14; Philem. 24; II Tim. 4:11).

Date of writing about A.D. 63, possibly while Paul was in prison in Caesarea (Acts 24:27).

The contents present a divinely edited account of the history of the early church.

2. THEME

While in his Gospel, Luke tells of what Jesus "began" to do, in the book of Acts, Luke tells of that which Jesus "continues" to do under the direction of the Holy Spirit, through the dedicated instrumentality of consecrated men and women.

The central theme is still "Christ," but now it is the risen, living, empowering Christ who challenges His believers to "go into all the world" with the matchless story of God's love.

3. MAIN DIVISIONS

(Acts 1:8) The "power" comes (1); the witness in Jerusalem (3-5); the witness in Judea (6: 7); the witness in Samaria (8); the witness to all the earth (9-28).

4. OUTLINE

The Church at Jerusalem
Prayer and Pentecost (1; 2)
First Miracle (3)
Growth, Persecution (4; 5)
Deacons (6)
Stephen (7)

The Church in Palestine
Phillip in Samaria (9)
Saul Converted (9)
Peter and Gentiles (10; 11)
Peter Delivered (12)

The Church of the Gentiles
First Missionary Tour (13; 14)
Council at Jerusalem (15)
Second Missionary Tour (15-18)
Third Missionary Tour (18-21)
Last Days of Paul (21-28)

5. SPECIAL CHARACTERISTICS

Here is God's pattern for His Church. The principles enunciated here furnish a norm for all Christian living, for all church activity, for all missionary procedure.

The book pulsates with a new life . . . that of the Holy Spirit. He is everywhere seen as the Director, Source of Power, Comforter, Edifier. The title could well be "The Acts of the Holy Spirit."

6. OUTSTANDING TEACHINGS

The day of Pentecost is the birthday of the Church.

Paul is our pattern too. Three times he is led to say, "Follow me as I follow Christ."

The Church's most important decision of all time . . . salvation is by grace through faith, not of works (see chapter 15).

The Church is missions, and missions is the Church. These can never be separated. The group of believers at Antioch is a sample (see 13:1-4; 14:26-28).

7. KEY TO UNDERSTANDING

This important book is God's great instruction volume for procedure and advance. All Christians, all churches, all missionary societies and Christian enterprises should know its principles thoroughly.

This is the greatest book of missions in the world. It is also the greatest book on church organization and procedure. Nor should missions and the church be separated. Neither one is complete without the other.

Romans

1. BACKGROUND

Writer, Paul the Apostle, who is also the human author of at least 12 other books in the New Testament. Written from Corinth and carried by one named Phoebe (16:1) who was traveling to Rome. Date is about A.D. 57 just previous to Paul's departure for Judea to complete his third missionary journey.

Occasion: Paul intended to visit Rome in the near

future, and wrote to prepare the way for his coming. Perhaps also in his mind was the thought that if he did not arrive, the church there might have the great foundational truths of the Gospel.

2. THEME

Doctrinally Romans is the greatest book ever written. It is the heart and soul of God's revelation to the people of this age. The entire body of redemption truth called in Scripture "the Gospel" is herein detailed. The most complete story of the need, the remedy, and the results of the death of Christ is found in Romans. The key thought is the righteousness of God. The key verse is 1:16. The progression of truth is from utter condemnation to complete and righteous glorification.

3. MAIN DIVISIONS

Romans is the soul of consistency. It begins with condemnation, and proceeds through salvation, justification, sanctification (then a section on dispensational truth reconciling God's promises to Israel with God's promises to the church), ending with glorification.

4. OUTLINE

Introduction
Salutation (1)
Personal Interest (1)
Purpose (1)
Sin's Condemnation
Gentiles (1)
Jews (2)
Christ's Salvation
Abraham (4)
Justification (5)
Santification (6; 7)
Adoption (8)

Israel's Program
Election (9)
Rejection (10)
Restoration (11)
Consecration
Personal Purity (12)
Social Submission (13)
Brotherly Love (14)
Conclusion
Personal Plans (15)
Greetings (16)
Doxology (16)

5. SPECIAL CHARACTERISTICS

While Romans is an epistle (letter) it is most carefully

and systematically written. It seems to present a courtroom scene with mankind on trial before Almighty God.

Time and time again Paul presents the tremendous questions of life and proceeds to answer them in the truth of God.

The entire orbit of truth is traversed beginning with man in a state of utter hopelessness and helplessness and ending with him as a Son of the living God, absolutely righteous and possessing eternal life.

The complete answer to the all-important question of Israel's program and future is superbly dealt with in chapters 9 through 11.

6. OUTSTANDING TEACHINGS

The most solemn, awe-inspiring, soul-chilling words ever written are found in 1:18-32. Here God deliberately condemns an entire universe.

The hinge point of Romans is between 3:20 and 3:21 where Paul shows that righteousness is now possible entirely apart from the merit principle.

Great, mighty, overwhelming truths are enunciated in chapters 4-7. This is some of the "strong meat" (Heb. 5:14) of the Bible.

One of the greatest mountain peaks of Scripture is Romans 8. Here is introduced the Holy Spirit as the believer's Helper. Whereas in chapter 7 the emphasis had been on the Christian's own strength which ended in complete failure, at the end of chapter 8 the believer is exultant in glorious victory through the power of the Spirit.

The vital question concerning the future of God's ancient people, the Jews, is completely and satisfactorily answered in chapters 9-11. Also, the uneasy query: If God had broken His covenant with Israel, would He keep it with the Church?

The last five chapters are blessed and practical, showing the outflow of the truths of the Gospel.

7. KEY TO UNDERSTANDING

You may read Romans straight through for it is completely logical. You would do well to read it thoughtfully 25 times, letting the teaching take hold of your life. This book will give you strength.

I Corinthians

1. BACKGROUND

Writer, Paul (Acts 18:1-18); place of writing is Ephesus, about A.D. 59, near the close of Paul's ministry there (20:31). Corinth was a city in southern Greece, rich, populous, and highly immoral. Paul had visited there for 18 months, establishing a large church.

After Paul had left, numerous questions arose as to life and conduct. Paul had heard rumors (1:11) and had received a letter asking questions (7:1). Hence this letter to the Corinthian church, dealing with practical matters of the Christian life.

2. THEME

The subject is Christian living. Sincerely and frankly the apostle deals with factions in the church, immoral conduct of one of its members, lawsuits against Christians, marriage and divorce. Christian liberty, separation from sinners, conduct at the Lord's Table, distribution and exercise of spiritual gifts, problems connected with the gift of tongues, truth of the resurrection. It is easy to feel the grief, solicitude, and holy indignation the apostle feels on these vital matters of conduct.

3. MAIN DIVISIONS

There can be no rigid analysis of the contents of I Corinthians. The apostle takes one subject after another and deals with it.

The divisions are the topics under discussion.

4. OUTLINE

Introduction (1:1-9)
Divisions Deplored
  (1:10-4:21)
Discipline Directed
  (5; 6)
Difficulties Discussed
  (7-11)

Spiritual Gifts (12-14)
The Resurrection (15)
Conclusion (16)

5. SPECIAL CHARACTERISTICS

It should be noted that chapter 1, verse 2, shows the scope of this practical letter to be "all that in every place call upon the name of Jesus Christ."

While it is true that Paul speaks in true affection, still there is an utter absence of compromise. He "pulls no punches" nor does ho "soft pedal" any basic truth. With error of any kind, Paul is a stern taskmaster.

Interposed between many of Paul's corrective teachings is positive doctrine such as (1) the truth about the Christian's rewards (3:11-15); (2) the teaching about the Holy Spirit's indwelling (6:19, 20); (3) the mystery of the rapture of the Church (15:51, 52).

6. OUTSTANDING TEACHINGS

What contempt and shame Paul pours on the divisions forming in the church 1:11-17: Is Christ divided?

Corinth was a center of worldly wisdom. But the cross of Christ is the antithesis of worldly wisdom. Chapters 1 and 2 deal thoroughly with this.

The question of meat offered to idols serves as an illustration for a vital Christian life principle. Can we afford to do anything, even though it may appear to be innocent, or harmless, if such a practice harms a weaker brother?

The important subject of the Lord's Table had evidently became the subject of a special revelation from the Lord to Paul. In chapter 11 he severely rebukes disorders there, and warns concerning who may partake.

The subject of "spiritual gifts," especially the matter of the gift of "tongues," is satisfactorily dealt with in 12-14.

Another mountain peak is the lovely chapter 15 about the Resurrection.

7. KEY TO UNDERSTANDING

Just understand I Corinthians for what it is, God's answer to many problems in the Christian life. There are some basic principles here too.

II Corinthians

1. BACKGROUND

Writer, the Apostle Paul, who signs his name as he begins the letter (1:1); date is about A.D. 60, and the place of writing, Macedonia.

The occasion: Paul had written the first Corinthian letter from Ephesus. Then he had left Ephesus due to a great riot (Acts 19) and had come to Macedonia. In the meantime, he had dispatched Titus to go to Corinth to aid in straightening out affairs in that church. While waiting for word from Titus, he was full of anxiety and concern. When Titus rejoined him in Macedonia he brought tidings that Paul's letter had done great good. Soon he wrote II Corinthians and sent it again by the hand of Titus.

2. THEME

The subject is that of the problems at hand. First, there is additional counsel for the Corinthian church. Then, due to the fact that much criticism had arisen regarding Paul's apostleship, he writes to vindicate his position, showing that he was indeed God's messenger for this hour. In addition, he bares his own sacrificial life in behalf of the churches and tells of his joy in service despite the rigors and hardships of the ministry.

3. MAIN DIVISIONS

Paul's principles of action (1-7); the collection for the saints (8;9); Paul's defense of his apostolic ministry (10-13).

4. OUTLINE

Introduction
  Salutation (1)
  Thanksgiving (1)
Vindication of Ministry
  Sincerity (1)
  Absence Explained (2)
  Living Epistles (3)
  Tribulation (4)
  Conduct (5)
  Consolation (7)
Jerusalem Collection
  Macedonian Liberty (8)

  Titus Commissioned (8)
  Bounties and Blessings (9)
Vindication of Authority
  Spiritual Power (10)
  Labors and Sufferings (11)
  Glory in Infirmities (12)
Conclusion
  Discipline Determined (13)
  Examination Exhorted (13)
  Farewell (13)

5. SPECIAL CHARACTERISTICS

This letter is the most personal of all Paul's letters. It discloses the great pain and weariness of the apostle due to the magnitude of his task in evangelization and the burden of the churches.

II Corinthians is partially Paul's autobiography. In it he discloses things not mentioned elsewhere. For instance: his thorn in the flesh and the reason (12:7); his remarkable visions (12:1-4); the extraordinary privations he endured (11:23-27).

There seems to be no orderly arrangements of the contents. It is largely emotional and throbs with the sense of Paul's personal anguish. Here and there we find an impassioned self-defense because of unjust charges being brought against him.

Some sidelights on the appearance of Paul are hinted at in 10:9, 10; 11:5, 6.

6. OUTSTANDING TEACHINGS

The sequel to the judgment for the immoral person found in Paul's first letter is a happy one. Evidently there was genuine repentance which brought forgiveness and restoration (2:1-13).

A large addition to the information as to what happens at death is given in chapter 5. Perhaps this subject weighed heavily on Paul's mind at this time.

The central passage on the grace of giving is found in chapters 8 and 9. There the secret of joy in giving is found to be in first giving one's own self to the Lord.

A rather startling revelation of the deceitful strategy of Satan is taught in 11:13-15.

The important matter of separation from the world is taught in 6:11-18.

7. KEY TO UNDERSTANDING

It is very important to know the background of the letter and read it with your heart full of sympathy and admiration for this great man of God.

Galatians

1. BACKGROUND

Writer, Paul; time is about A.D. 57; the place of writing undoubtedly Corinth. The Galatians were citizens of certain sections of Asia Minor, near the Black Sea (see Acts 13; 14).

Occasion; Paul had evangelized these people, and they had gladly received the word of the Gospel. After Paul left, there had come Judaizing teachers endeavoring to show that Christianity was sort of an exalted Judaism, and that every Christian must also keep the law. The Galatians were following them, and were turning aside from the truth of the Gospel.

2. THEME

Galatians is the Great Magna Charta, or Declaration of Independence of the Gospel. The key word is "liberty." The key verse is 5:11. This book is closely related to Romans, but the emphasis is somewhat different. In Galatians the stress is on the fact that the Christian LIVES by faith. Here is an Emancipation Proclamation to all who are in the bondage of the law.

3. MAIN DIVISIONS

Note seven main divisions: Salutation; theme; Paul's gospel a revelation; justification by faith without law; the believer's rule is grace, not law; sanctification through the Spirit now law; exhortation.

4. OUTLINE

Introduction [1]
Personal Authority
  Call (1)
  Endorsement (2)
  Controversy (2)
Gospel Authority
  Justification by Faith (3)

Purpose of the Law (3)
Servants and Heirs (4)
Personal Application
Law and Liberty (5)
Personal Responsibility (6)
Conclusion [6]

5. SPECIAL CHARACTERISTICS

This letter is severe in its tone. The theme is considered to be one of vital importance. There is not a single word of commendation given. Paul shows himself to be very indignant against the Galatians.

Paul considers this error (mixing grace and law) to be extremely dangerous. It is moreover, infectious. The reason, Paul thinks, is not ignorance but unfaithfulness.

Paul's usual custom in writing letters was to use a secretary. Here, however, he writes with his own hand (6:11). This may have been due to the seriousness of the matter before him.

The real trouble in Galatia was legalism. False teachers were endeavoring to combine Judaism with

Christianity. This is a subtle form of error. Paul calls this "another gospel" and roundly condemns it (1:7-9).

The character of the Galatians themselves seems to be that of being emotional, impulsive, and changeable. This is evidenced by their first worshiping Paul, and then suddenly changing and stoning him (Acts 14:13-19).

6. OUTSTANDING TEACHINGS

The tremendous importance of Paul's teachings is clearly indicated and repeated by the strong statement in verses 8 and 9 of chapter 1, where any other teaching is said to bring God's curse.

Nowhere in the Scriptures do we find stronger statements concerning the sufficiency of the grace message. Galatians is God's answer to the many cults of today which propose a mixture of Old and New Testament teachings.

Most clearly are we shown the true character of the law as Paul uses the term "schoolmaster" or "child conductor" in referring to its purpose (3:24, 25).

Other error can be prevented when we remember that to "fall from grace" (5:4) is to fall into law.

7. KEY TO UNDERSTANDING

Before you study Galatians, refresh yourself on Galatian history in Acts 13 and 14; then read again the book of Romans. Then you will be ready to read and understand Galatians.

Ephesians

1. BACKGROUND

Writer, Paul; time, probably A.D. 62; place of writing is Rome. Ephesians is one of the "prison epistles," i.e., written while Paul was imprisoned.

Ephesus was an important city in Asia Minor. It had a

theater that seated 50,000; its temple to Diana was one of the seven wonders of the world. Paul had visited there and stayed about 3 years, having an immense ministry among those people (Acts 19:10). Ephesus was the scene of much conflict. Paul relates that it was there that he had "fought with beasts" (I Cor. 15:32), there he had almost lost his life in the riot (Acts 20:1), yet loved the people dearly.

2. THEME

The subject is "the Church of which Christ is the Head." The important words are: "unity," "oneness," "in Christ," "edify." This is the most impersonal of all of Paul's writings. Paul seems not to be so much concerned about the local church as he is about the universal, true Church or the Body of Christ.

The most profound, sublime truth of the New Testament is here. Absent is the practical. Present is the heavenly, all transcendent, universal truth.

3. MAIN DIVISIONS

You may think of Ephesians in this way: What God has done for us (1-3); What we may do for God (4-6). Or, by chapters: Boundless (1)) limitless (2); measureless (3); fathomless (4); faultless (5); dauntless (6).

4. OUTLINE

Introduction (1)

Divine Origin

    Chosen, Redeemed (1)

    Enlightened, Human Inability (2)

    Spiritual Construction (2)

Gentile Constituency (3)

Rules of Conduct

    Charity, Unity (4)

    Purity, Family (4; 5)

Rules for Conflict (6)

Conclusion

5. SPECIAL CHARACTERISTICS

Some of the oldest manuscripts do not have "to the Ephesians." Because of this, some have thought this a circular letter to many churches round about Ephesus.

In the first three chapters there is not one exhortation. All that is there tells of God's limitless grace extended in the saint's behalf. Note the past tense used frequently.

There is a close relationship between Ephesians and the book of Joshua.

The Old Testament book illustrates the New Testament truth showing that in the Christian life there is conflict and often failure; but eventual victory, rest, and possession. The number "seven" is conspicuous in the structure.

In this letter, as in no other place in the Bible, we find the broad outline of the plan of God for all time (1:10; 2:7).

6. OUTSTANDING TEACHINGS

The highly exalted position of the simple believer in Christ is stressed by the use of the past tense to indicate accomplishment as "hath blessed' (1:3); "hath chosen" (1:4); "having predestinated" (1:5); etc.

Two lovely prayers right from the apostle's heart are seen in 1:15-23; 3:14-21. These may well be emulated by Spirit-taught believers today.

The doctrine of salvation, by grace through faith plus nothing, clearly portrayed in 2:8, 9.

The true character of peace showing it to be a Person, not a state of mind, is taught in 2:13.

The hopeless condition of the Gentile previous to the cross of Christ is graphically portrayed in verses 11 through 13 of chapter 2.

The true source of the believer's success is in the "filling of the Spirit" as exhorted in 5:18.

The order of the Christian life is illustrated here. First, God, for Christ's sake had already done amazing, eternal things for us. Now, if we care to, we may serve Him according to chapters 4-6.

7. KEY TO UNDERSTANDING

This is the "holiest of all." Read it on your knees, and don't restrain the tears of gratitude that may come. Remember, it's for you—even though just a new believer.

This is God's plan, and God will bring it to pass in your life, if you'll allow Him.

Philippians

1. BACKGROUND

Writer, Paul the Apostle; place of writing is Rome (prison); time, about A.D. 63.

This letter is written to a church in Philippi, an important city and a Roman colony (military center). The church had been founded by Paul some ten years earlier (Acts 16).

Occasion: Learning of Paul's imprisonment, the church took up an offering for him and sent it to Rome by the hand of a young man named Epaphroditus.

Philippians is the letter or "thank you note" which Paul wrote in appreciation to the church.

2. THEME

This letter is the most affectionate of all Paul's writings. It is free from censure and full of tenderness and expressions of love. The general subject seems to be that of rejoicing in spite of manifold testings. Key words are: "rejoice," "content," "joy," "peace." The key verse might be 4:4. The thought of God's overruling providence pervades the Epistle. Paul expresses it well in 1:21—"to live is Christ, and to die is gain."

3. MAIN DIVISIONS

Christ—the Life of Life (1); the Pattern of Life (2); the Goal of Life (3); the All-Sufficiency of Life (4). Another: Joy of Faith (1); Joy of Love (2); Joy of Communion (3); Joy of Hope (4).

4. OUTLINE

Introduction (1)
Gratitude
  Memory (1)
  Experience (1)
  Expectation (1)
Exhortation
  Unity (2)
  Humility (2)
  Cheerfulness (2)
Ministering Messengers (2)
Warning
  Legalism (3)
  False Liberty (3)
Rejoicing (4)
Conclusion (4)

5. SPECIAL CHARACTERISTICS

There is no reproof or correction for the church at Philippi. Evidently they were walking in the light of the truth of God for Paul expresses no anxiety or concern for them.

The term "joy" is the predominant note of the Epistle, being used 17 times. This quality is one of the fruit of the Spirit (Gal. 5:22, 23).

Paul promises to send his greatly beloved Timothy to the church (2:19-23) but also suggests that he may come himself shortly (2:24).

The "mailman" of the letter was Epaphroditus who almost lost his life through illness. Paul praises his faithfulness highly. While not strictly a "doctrinal" letter, some important teaching is woven into the structure, as for instance, foundation truth of giving and receiving (4:10-19), the example of Christ for our life of humility and exaltation (2:5-10).

6. OUTSTANDING TEACHINGS

Paul's great motto of life is evidently that of 1:21. It was no longer Paul who lived, or even Saul of Tarsus, but Christ who was all and in all.

Part of the "all things" of Rom. 8:28 for Paul was imprisonment (1:12, 13). Paul was in reality "prisoner of the Lord" in Rome.

The pattern of our life is evidently the pattern of the life of our Lord as given in 2:5-11. First the humiliation, then the exaltation.

The value of earthly achievements is treated in 3:4-14. In comparison with what we have in Christ, they are all loss.

A most gracious promise is 4:19, which in its wider application is able to encompass the entire Christian experience.

7. KEY TO UNDERSTANDING

Just remember that Paul was one of the Lord's own even though in prison. Then read the chapters ten times and you will not need to get hold of them—they will already have taken hold of you.

Colossians

1. BACKGROUND

Writer, Paul the Apostle; written from Rome in A.D. 62. Colossians is one of the "prison epistles."

The church was located in a city called Colosse, not far from Ephesus in Asia Minor. Evidently Paul had not personally established the church (2:1) but no doubt it had come from his ministry (Acts 19:10). Possibly, Epaphras (Col. 1:7) or even Archippus (4:17) had begun it.

Occasion: It is thought that Epaphras had come to Rome with news of a dangerous heresy making headway in the church. Subsequently, Epaphras was imprisoned too (Philem. 23). Paul, therefore, writes to the church sending the letter by way of Tychicus and Onesimus (Col. 4:7-9).

2. THEME

Colossians has a great theme . . . Christ the Head of the Church which is His body. It is closely related to Ephesians. Emphasis is strongly placed on the allness of the dear Son of God. Correction too, is taught. Pagan asceticism was creeping in, endeavoring to add its works to the finished ministry of Christ. Also, there were those suggesting mysticism, worship of angels, regard for the secret things. Paul answers all by a strong emphasis on the person of Christ.

3. MAIN DIVISIONS

Introduction: apostolic prayer; Christ . . . Creator, redeemer, indweller, believer complete in Christ; union with Christ in resurrection life and glory; Christian union, the fruit of union; Christian fellowship.

4. OUTLINE

Introduction (1:1-8)
Prayer (1:9-12)
Exposition —
Christ (1:13-29)
  Redeemer
  Reconciler
  Perfector
Admonition (2)
  False Doctrine
  Angel Worship

Exhortation (3:1-4:6)
  Holiness
  Charity
  Submission
  Sincerity
  Prayer
  Practice
Conclusion (4:7-18)

5. SPECIAL CHARACTERISTICS

The answer to error in the church is the preaching of a definite, specific message. The Colossians were taught to put the Lord Jesus Christ in the center of all they were doing.

Some worldly things which are often held in high repute . . . philosophic speculation, mysticism, aceticism, legality, worship of angels, are all shown in their true light. They are not for the child of God. In Christ, in His person and work, we find everything we need.

No greater honor to the person of Christ is found anywhere else in the New Testament. Christ is shown here in all the glory of His creative, redemptive work, possessing all the fullness of the Godhead.

6. OUTSTANDING TEACHINGS

The problem here seemed to be the attainment of sanctification. Paul shows this already true positionally

(2:10) and true experimentally by a close walk with Christ (2:6).

The dangers of philosophical education apart from Christ are shown (2:8) to be tradition of men and therefore, valueless. One of several great passages emphasizing the creatorhood of Christ is here (1:15-19). This passage shows further the reason for the creation. It is "for Him," that "He might have the pre-eminence."

Things which are to be put off (3:8, 9) by the Christian, and things which are to be put on (3:12-14) are specifically mentioned here.

One of the great principles of Christian conduct, covering many specific and individual life problems, is mentioned in 3:17. Related to this verse is I Corinthians 10:31.

The interweaving of doctrine and practice is again demonstrated in this Epistle. The method is to know the teaching and find it unconsciously influencing your Christian conduct.

7. KEY TO UNDERSTANDING

Just write across every verse in Colossians "Complete in Christ" and understand that you need nothing more. Let your manner of life demonstrate this by a daily reliance on the Word of Christ (3:16).

I Thessalonians

1. BACKGROUND

Writer, Paul; time of writing about A.D. 52; place of writing, Corinth during Paul's first visit there (Acts 18).

Thessalonica (present-day Saloniki) was a large and important city of Macedonia on the main Roman highway. Evidently, there was a large colony of Jews there, and Paul had founded a church there as he traveled from Philippi (Acts 17:1-9).

Soon after the church was established, Paul had to

leave. But he was anxious about the church's welfare and finally sent Timothy to learn if all was well (I Thess. 3:1-5). Timothy returned with news of the church's condition and this letter is the result (Acts 18:5).

2. THEME

The outstanding subject is the return of Christ. Because Paul's ministry in Thessalonica had been somewhat brief, there was necessity to confirm the young believers in the truths Paul had already given them. Coupled wtith this is an exhortation to holiness of life, encouragement in spite of persecution (3:2-4), and comfort to those who had lost loved ones in death (4:1-13).

3. MAIN DIVISIONS

Three tenses of the Christian life (1); rewards to the model servant (2); the believer's sanctification (3); the believer's hope (4); the coming day of the Lord (5).

4. OUTLINE

Introduction (1)

Reminiscences (2; 3)
  Preaching, Persecution
  Timothy, Consolation

Exhortation (4:1-12)
  Purity, Charity

Exposition (4:13-5:3)
  Advent of Christ
  Uncertainty of Time

Application (5:4-22)
  Comfort, Conduct

Conclusion (5:23-28)

5. SPECIAL CHARACTERISTICS

Each chapter ends with a special message as to the Lord's return.

This letter (and II Thess.) are the earliest of Paul's writings.

Paul's success in Thessalonica was remarkable. Among his converts were Deman (II Tim. 4:10), Gaius (Acts 19:29), Secundus (20:4), Aristarchus (27:2; Col. 4:10).

We are not sure if Paul ministered in Thessalonica only about a month (Acts 17:2) or if he ministered further in the house of Jason (v. 5). At any rate, the teaching during that time included such doctrines as: election, Holy Spirit, assurance, Trinity, conversion, second coming of Christ, believer's walk, sanctification, day of the Lord, resurrection, threefold nature of man.

The Christians at Thessalonica evidently had formed a strong affection and attachment for their Teacher as evidenced by 3:6-10.

Paul's work in Thessalonica was remarkable for his enemies accused him of "turning the world upside down" (Acts 17:6). This work was heralded all over Greece (I Thess. 1:8, 9).

6. OUTSTANDING TEACHINGS

The true motion of the Christian life (1:9) is turning to God, **from** idols. Not, from idols to God.

The influence of just one church is stated in 1:8 how that the Church of the Thessalonians had a worldwide reputation for faith.

The necessity of sexual purity is stressed in 4:1-5 in the midst of a civilization that was loose-living in the extreme.

Central passage on the rapture of the church is found in 4:13-18 where Paul reveals the glorious details of the coming of Christ for His own. These are words divinely given for comfort.

Teaching on the high regard for faithful ministers stems from 5:12, 13.

Brief sevenfold admonition for Christian living given in 5:16-22.

7. KEY TO UNDERSTANDING

I Thessalonians will be best understood as teaching Christian living from the standpoint of the nearness of the Lord's return. We should live as if Christ died yesterday, arose this morning, and was returning tomorrow.

II Thessalonians

1. BACKGROUND

Writer, the Apostle Paul who pens this letter from

Corinth about A.D. 52 (as with also the first epistle to the Thessalonians).

Paul had established the church there as he came from Troas and Philippi on his second missionary journey (Acts 17). But he had been driven from the city and had gone on south to Berea, Athens, and Corinth. However, he was much concerned about the infant church in Thessalonica and he sent his friend, Timothy, to return and observe. In due time Timothy reported that all was well, and the church was growing. Paul here wrote I Thessalonians and sent it by the hand of Timothy.

It is thought that II Thessalonians was sent soon after by the same messenger.

2. THEME

The subject of this second letter is still the return of Christ. But the Thessalonian Christians were "shaken in mind and troubled" mostly due to a forged letter purported to have come from Paul, telling them that the present persecutions were the beginning of the great and terrible day of the Lord. This was in contrast to what Paul had previously taught, that they were to be delivered from this hour of trial. This second letter to the Thessalonians then, is written to clarify doctrine already given.

3. MAIN DIVISIONS

The letter can be divided as: comfort (1); instruction (2); exhortation (3).

4. OUTLINE

Introduction (1:1-5)
Instruction (1:6-2:12)
  Day of Judgment
  Man of Sin

Application (2:13-3:15)
  Consolation
  Prayer
  Labor
  Obedience
Conclusion (3:16-18)

5. SPECIAL CHARACTERISTICS

The first letter to the Thessalonians was written to "comfort;" the second letter to "correct."

Both letters are marked with simplicity and great affection. They show deep affection and love which does not always characterize Paul's later letters.

It is noteworthy that there are no direct quotations from the Old Testament which could be due to the fact that Paul is addressing Gentile believers who knew nothing of the older Scriptures.

6. OUTSTANDING TEACHINGS

Evidently the teaching here has the main thought of the coming of Christ in power and great glory; this is in distinction to the emphasis in I Thessalonians which is on the rapture or translation of the Church.

A strong passage in chapter 2:3-12 tells of many characteristics of the coming man of sin, who is also called the beast, the son of perdition, and the antichrist.

The words translated "let" and "letteth" in 2:7 are better understood by the margin rendering of "hinder" and "hindereth" and no doubt refer to the work of the Holy Spirit in this age. It seems that there were some in Thessalonica who understood the truth of the nearness of the Lord's return to be a signal for them to quit their jobs and wait for Him in idleness. To these Paul directs strong commands that "work and eat their own bread." Added to this were stern directions that if any did not obey the word of the apostle, he was to be ostracized from the Christian company.

While the second coming of Christ was to Paul the "blessed hope" (Titus 2:13), yet he never permitted the imminence to interfere with his ardent and fervent labors for Christ.

7. KEY TO UNDERSTANDING

In your mind you may associate these two books together. They both deal largely with the coming of Christ. Read them with your eyes shining.

I Timothy

1. BACKGROUND

Writer, Paul; time of writing is A.D. 65 from Macedonia (North Greece).

Letter is written to Timothy, a dear friend of Paul and pastor of the church of Ephesus. Paul had found young Timothy at Lystra (Acts 16:1-3) and had chosen him to be his assistant. Of him Paul wrote, "I have no man likeminded" (Phil. 2:20), for he had become the most intimate and trusted friend Paul possessed.

Occasion: Evidently Paul had been released from his first Roman imprisonment and had revisited Ephesus and had gone to Macedonia, leaving Timothy there. As he went he wrote this book of pastoral instruction about the work Timothy was to do.

2. THEME

I Timothy is one of three (also II Tim., Titus) "pastoral epistles." The subject is order, organization, procedure in the churches. At the first, all the problems in the churches were handled by the apostles directly. But as the end of the apostolic era approached, it was necessary that the Spirit of God write down a clear revelation for the guidance in future churches.

3. MAIN DIVISIONS

Unsound doctrine rebuked (1); prayer and the divine order (2); qualifications of elders and deacons (3); walk of a good minister (4); work of a good minister (5).

4. OUTLINE

Introduction (1:1, 2)
False Teachers (1:3-20)
  Prayer
  Conduct
Church Officers (3)
Minister
Deacon
Church Government (4-6)
Minister
Congregation
Conclusion (6:20, 21)

5. SPECIAL CHARACTERISTICS

Timothy was a comparatively young man, but one of whom nothing derogatory is written. He was ordained an evangelist (4:14; II Tim. 1:6), was not in best of health (5:23), was Paul's most trusted and beloved companion, and after Paul's death and on the completion of his ministry in the Ephesian church, suffered martyrdom under the Emperor Domitian.

Timothy's work was possibly mostly with pastors. As there were no seminaries in which to teach pastors, it was necessary to develop them out of the converts. This was done in spite of the persecution and lack of facilities of that early day. How Timothy came to be the fine young man he was is somewhat explained by II Timothy 1:5; 3:14, 15. Though his father was a Greek, his mother was a Jewess and evidently carefully and prayerfully instructed her son in the faith, being ably assisted by Timothy's grandmother as well.

It would be remembered that at this time there were no church buildings. Possibly the church at Ephesus met in the homes of the Christians there. These may have numbered in the scores. Timothy may have acted as general Pastor teaching other local leaders.

6. OUTSTANDING TEACHINGS

I Timothy's greatest problem was false teachers (Acts 20:29, 30). Their line of falsehood dealt with Jewish legends and endless genealogies.

Paul writes carefully of women's place in the church. While in heaven there will be no distinction, still in the church there are natural differences which it is best not to override. Clear, definite qualifications are laid down for the officers of the church in all ages. All of this is in direct contrast with the practice of selecting men to rule the church by their worldly ahcievements or position.

Teaching on slavery: become free if you can, but if not, be the very best slave you possibly can . . . for Christ's sake. Riches produce opportunity for corruption. Don't desire them.

7. KEY TO UNDERSTANDING

You'll find here God's own instruction for pastors, for church leaders, and for every member of the church.

II Timothy

1. BACKGROUND

Writer, Paul, time is about A.D. 67; place of writing is Rome.

Timothy, to whom the letter was written, was Paul's dear son in the faith.

II Timothy is closely related to the first letter to Timothy. It is believed that after Paul left Timothy at Ephesus (I Tim. 1:3) and Titus at Crete (Titus 1:5) he went on to Macedonia where I Timothy was written. Possibly Paul then visited several other churches he had promised to visit. Soon Paul was arrested and taken to Rome where he was again imprisoned. As he awaited his trial (4:16-18) he sent this heart-filled letter to his beloved Timothy urging him to come to him quickly (4:21).

2. THEME

This letter was Paul's last message to his children in the faith. The subject seems to be the walk and warfare of a good soldier of Jesus Christ. The one speaking is the old warrior who was about to go off the scene. He wrote to encourage many to follow him, and voiced his final shout of triumph.

3. MAIN DIVISIONS

The apostle's greeting (1); the right way in a day of apostasy (2); apostasy and the Word (3); a faithful servant and his faithful Lord (4).

4. OUTLINE

Introduction (1:1-5)
Christian Conduct
  (1:6-2:14)

Christian Preaching
  (2:15-4:5)
  Preparation

Courage	Congregation
Steadfastness	Scripturalism
Endurance	Dispensation

Paul's Last Words (4:6-22)

5. SPECIAL CHARACTERISTICS

Though this letter does not mention this, it was at this time that the great fire in Rome occurred. And Nero, in order to divert suspicion from himself, accused the Christians of the crime.

In Paul's first imprisonment he had been allowed to stay in his own hired house (Acts 28:30). But with his re-arrest, he was confined to the infamous Mammertime Prison in the city of Rome itself.

It is possible that Alexander, the Ephesian copper-smith, was largely instrumental in Paul's arrest and trial (4:14; Acts 19:33).

Not only does Paul urge Timothy three times to come to him, but the dankness of the prison can be visualized as he pleads for the cloak (4:13) which he left at Troas, and the books and the parchments.

Paul's only companion was his faithful "beloved physician" Luke. Some of his friends had forsaken him under the pressure. Others, he had sent in the line of duty. Now he calls also for John Mark, who helped Paul in his early ministry, had subsequently failed, and later proved himself to be worthy (4:11).

6. OUTSTANDING TEACHINGS

Here is Paul's valedictory. Here are the last utterances of the greatest Christian who ever lived. The battle-scarred warrior looking back over his lone and busy life cries out "I have kept the faith."

While I Timothy seems concerned about the work of a pastor, II Timothy emphasized the work of the preacher. There was need of courage, steadfastness, and fidelity, especially since many were departing from the faith.

Paul looks into the future and exhorts Timothy to "endure hardness," to commit the testimony to faithful men, to study to show himself approved unto God.

Perilous times were ahead and there were to be trials and persecutions for all who would live godly in Christ Jesus.

7. KEY TO UNDERSTANDING

These last words ought to be read in connection with Paul's outline-autobiography in II Corinthians 11:16-33. Here indeed was God's man, the greatest defender of the Gospel who ever lived. Read this and go out to do likewise.

Titus

1. BACKGROUND

Writer, the Apostle Paul; the place, Macedonia about A.D. 65.

Titus was one of Paul's trusted helpers. He was a Greek, possibly a native of Syrian Antioch. He was used largely in Paul's ministry to Corinth (II Cor. 2:13; 7:6; 8:23). Evidently on Paul's release from his first Roman imprisonment, Titus joined him. Soon Paul left him to stay in Crete (Titus 1:5) while he, Paul, went on to Macedonia. While in Macedonia Paul wrote this letter along with the first letter to Timothy.

We last hear of Titus (II Tim. 4; 10) as Paul sends him to minister to the churches in Dalmatia (N.W. coast of Greece).

2. THEME

This book has much in common with I Timothy. The subject matter is the "work of the pastor." Titus was charged to ordain elders, and to train the constituency. There is perhaps a twofold application: first to correct churches who had grown careless as to the truth of God; then, to correct churches who had become lax as to the order of God's house. Here is the divine order for churches of all times.

3. MAIN DIVISIONS

The qualifications and functions of an elder (1); the pastoral work of a true elder (2; 3).

4. OUTLINE

Introduction	Conduct in home
Christian Officers (1:5-16)	Aged
Elder	Young
Bishop	Servants
False Teachers	General
Christian Instruction	Conduct in Society
(2:1-3:11)	**Conclusion** (3:12-15)

5. SPECIAL CHARACTERISTICS

It is possible that the church in Crete was founded by one of the converts from the day of Pentecost (Acts 2:11). Also, it is implied that Paul himself had visited and evangelized on the island.

The Cretians were thought to be akin to the Philistines. They were daring sailors and famous bowmen but with a very bad moral reputation. In Paul's day many Jews lived there.

The degree of civilization in Crete was not too high. One of their own poets called them "liars, evil beasts, idlo gluttons." But Paul felt sure the power of the Gospel could transform lives there too.

Evidently Paul did not purpose that Titus should settle down permanently in Crete but that he might be relieved by either Artemas or Tychicus, for he instructs Titus to meet him at Nicopolis (3:12) where he intended to winter.

6. OUTSTANDING TEACHINGS

The terms "Elder" and "Bishop" are synonymous. One emphasized the person and the other the office. Very strict and rigid qualifications are required, for this is a most important office in the Church of the living God.

The problem of false teachers is again dealt with (1:10-16) with the term "whole houses" meaning whole churches. The mouths of the unruly and deceivers were to be stopped by a vigorous proclamation of the truth.

Strong emphasis is given here on "good works," not as a means of salvation, but as an evidence. (See 2:7; 2:14; 3:1; 3:8).

The power of beautiful lives is shown to be a complete answer to the critics of the Gospel (2:8).

Here is the place in the New Testament where the rapture of the church is spoken of as "the blessed hope" (2:11-14), and is a compelling motive for godly living.

The "genealogies" referred to evidently concerned false teachers seeking to prove Davidic lineage, or to claim kinship with Christ.

7. KEY TO UNDERSTANDING

Put yourself in Titus' place as a pastor laboring under difficult circumstances. This letter is instruction from your teacher.

Philemon

1. BACKGROUND

Writer, Paul; written about A.D. 64 from Rome.

Philemon was a Christian gentleman, a member of the church of Colosse. He was a well-to-do man and possibly the church met in his house. It seems that he was an intimate friend of Paul.

Occasion: Onesimus, a slave of Philemon, had apparently stolen money and fled to Rome. While there he somehow met Paul. After Onesimus received Christ, Paul told him to return to his master Philemon.

Paul writes this letter to Philemon asking forgiveness for Onesimus and sends it by him. This is one of the "prison epistles."

2. THEME

This is purely a personal letter dealing with a domestic matter. Out of all the voluminous mail of Paul, this letter alone is preserved for our edification. Not only is the subject matter dealt with, but the teaching of the letter constitutes a lovely, tender, sincere example of the outworkings of the grace of God in the heart of a Christian.

3. MAIN DIVISIONS

Greeting (vv. 1-3); character of Philemon (4-7); appeal for Onesimus (8-21); salutations (22-25).

4. OUTLINE

Greetings (1-3)　　　　　Brotherly Love
Thanksgiving (4-7)　　　**Conclusion** (22-25)
Purpose (8-21)　　　　　Hope of Release
　　Paul　　　　　　　　　Salutations
　　Onesimus

5. SPECIAL CHARACTERISTICS

"Apphia" (v. 2) was no doubt the wife of Philemon; "Archippus" was either his son or the local pastor.

There is a planned play on words in verse 11, as the name Onesimus means "profitable."

The use of the word "forever" in verse 15 was a hint of the extension of earthly friendships throughout eternity.

This letter is a perfect gem of tact, delicacy, courtesy, and generosity as Paul pleads for Philemon to receive Onesimus "as you would receive me."

There is no hint in Scripture as to how Philemon received Onesimus. However, tradition has it that he not only took him back, but, taking Paul's hint, gave Onesimus his freedom.

There is a tradition that Onesimus became a bishop in the Greek city of Berea, as mentioned by a writer, some years later.

6. OUTSTANDING TEACHINGS

Paul styles himself a "prisoner of Jesus Christ," not a prisoner of the Roman government or of Nero. This is in keeping with his conviction that God had placed him in Rome for a special ministry (Philem. 1:12).

There is no doubt that Philemon was not only a Christian brother, but a dear, good, generous, benevolent man of God. No doubt he was a large source of evangelism, and edification in Colosse. The close relationship of all believers in Christ is beautifully taught by Paul's new kinship to Onesimus. He is called Paul's "son" (v. 10).

Even though as a Christian Onesimus was now truly free, still Paul was careful to send him back directly to his former life. The miracle of salvation is not designed to produce a revolution, but a complete regeneration of the heart.

Paul's offer to "repay" what Onesimus had stolen is one of the most touching incidents in the New Testament (v. 18).

The fulfillment of Paul's promise to come and visit Philemon (v. 22) is thought to have been accomplished between his first and second Roman imprisonments.

7. KEY TO UNDERSTANDING

A tender illustration of how the Gospel operates in hearts and results in good deeds.

Hebrews

1. BACKGROUND

Writer, unknown. Many Bible scholars believe Paul wrote this book; time; about A.D. 65; written from Rome (13:24).

Occasion: The Gospel produced many converts from Judaism. Yet, up to A.D. 70 the religion of the Jews continued (10:11) as before the cross. The new Christians were severly persecuted and ostracized, so much so that many of them despaired, and contemplated turning back to Judaism. To counteract this tendency, the Holy Spirit encourages and confirms by the truth of this book.

2. THEME

Christ is the inevitable, the indispensable, the perfectly unique Person. He is better (word used 13 times), than anything or anyone. He is the fulfillment of all that the Old Testament promised. Without Him, all Old Testament persons and institutions are empty and pointless. To turn away from Him is to forsake life. So, do not allow yourselves to become discouraged under persecution. Rather you must press on to perfection. And our great High Priest, who is the Lord Jesus Christ, now at God's right hand, will aid you. Your efficient weapon is "faith."

3. MAIN DIVISIONS

There are six divisions which include five parenthetic passages of special exhortation: The great salvation (1; 2); the rest of God (3; 4); our Great High Priest (5-8); the New Covenant (9; 10); the way of faith (11); the Believer-Priest (12; 13).

4. OUTLINE

Superiority of Christ (1-7)
    Prophets, Angels
    Moses, High Priest
Superiority of Christianity (8-10)
    Covenant, Worship
    Fellowship

Witness (11)
    Heroes of Faith
    Perfector of Faith
Exhortation (12; 13:1-7)
    Conduct before God
    Conduct before Men
Conclusion (13:8-25)

5. SPECIAL CHARACTERISTICS

The pressure put on the early Hebrew Christians was tremendous. Zealous rabbis did everything short of murder in their effort to bring back Christian converts to the Jewish religion. To persecution and threats, they added arguments, remonstrances, and entreaties based on the excellencies of Judaism.

No New Testament book contains so many warnings. The word "lest" is used seven times to introduce the danger (2:1; 3:12; 13: 4:11; 12:3, 13, 15, 16). Apostacy, or turning away, is shown to be the blackest sin one can commit.

6. OUTSTANDING TEACHINGS

The first four verses comprise one of the grandest passages in the Bible.

Some consider chapter 11 as the greatest passage in all of the Scriptures.

Hebrews is the greatest Book in the Bible to encourage believers in the faith and to challenge them to "go on" to mature perfection.

While the Gospels and Acts emphasize the finished work of Christ, this Book emphasizes the "unfinished" work, going on day by day at God's right hand (7:25).

7. KEY TO UNDERSTANDING

Hebrews is written to Christians who, under stress or difficulty, are tempted to turn back. This is God's divinely given basis of encouragement.

James

1. BACKGROUND

Writer, James, a half brother of Jesus (Mark 6:3); apparently converted by the appearance of the risen Christ (I Cor. 15:7). James was present at the prayer gathering (Acts 1:14), later became pastor and teacher of the church at Jerusalem (Gal. 2:9). He was moderator of the Council at Jerusalem (Acts 15:13) and according to tradition, died a martyr's death there.

Written about A.D. 45 from Jerusalem.

Occasion: James writes to the "twelve tribes scattered abroad" by which he does not mean Jewish tribes, but Christian Jews of the dispersion, or foreign churches composed of Christian Jews. No doubt these Christians had written to the home church about their problems.

This letter may be the result. At any rate, the truth is elementary, yet basic and sound.

2. THEME

The emphasis is "works" and "holy living." Or, that a holy life and good works are the inevitable results of the Christian profession. It is not that salvation is other than by faith, but that true faith will certainly show its genuineness by good works in the life of the believer.

3. MAIN DIVISIONS

By chapters: Testing of faith (1; 2); an example of the reality of faith (3); rebuke of worldliness (4); rich warned (5).

4. OUTLINE

Introduction (1:1)
Trial of Faith (1:2-27)
  Temptation
    Purpose and Source
  Practical Rules
    Attention, Action
    Sincerity
Working of Faith (2)
  Respect of Persons
  Faith and Works

Wisdom of Faith (3)
  Tongue Trouble
  True Wisdom
Character of Faith (4)
  Purity, Charity
  Submission
Triumph of Faith (5:1-18)
  Oppression Avenged
  Patience Rewarded
  Prayer Answered
Conclusion (5:19, 20)

5. SPECIAL CHARACTERISTICS

The letter abounds in vivid imagery. With a single stroke, the writer commends a duty, scourges a fault, denounces a wrong, crowns a virtue.

There is a vast difference between the writing of Paul and James. The latter writes more of a treatise than an epistle. Without salvation or personal mention, James launches immediately into his subject and concludes with the climax of a platform speaker.

The book seems to be composed of detached subjects without apparent connection: Temptation, patience, wisdom, prayer, poverty, riches, lust, sin, faith, good works, respect of persons, the tongue, self-sufficiency.

The style and general content of the book seem to be related to the "wisdom books" of the Old Testament (Proverbs).

6. OUTSTANDING TEACHINGS

In Paul's writings we see the **principles** of salvation and faith, while in the epistle of James we see the very practical **outworking** of these principles.

It is easy to understand the need for the "Essay on the Tongue" as given in chapter 3. One can see presumptuous, worldly-minded men putting themselves forward to be leaders in the early church. In 2:8 we have the "royal law" given. The opposite is given next as having respect of persons which James denounces.

James divides wisdom between that which is "devilish" (3:15), and that which is "from above" or divine (3:17). Encouragement to sing is in 5:13.

7. KEY TO UNDERSTANDING

Salvation is a definite miracle of God and results in a transformed life. Some of the transformations are listed in James' letter.

I Peter

1. BACKGROUND

Writer, Peter the disciple-apostle (Matt. 10:2), brother of Andrew, spokesman of the Twelve and commanding figure in the early church.

Time of writing, about A.D. 65; written from Babylon on the river Euphrates (5:13).

Occasion: Peter writes to Jewish Christians of the dispersion (1:1), but also the Gentile Church (2:10) is included. The faith of the early Christians was being severely tested by manifold persecutions. They were also in extreme poverty. Peter writes to comfort.

2. THEME

The distinctive note is that of "victory over suffering." The turth is, that this is the order of the Christian life . . . the suffering and then the glory (4:13). The word suffering appears 15 times. Peter writes also for Christians to live blamelessly before magistrates so that their enemies' charges of sedition and lawlessness may be shown to be baseless. He also suggests that Paul's teachings (II Pet. 3:15, 16) are Scripture truth. Key word is "hope."

3. MAIN DIVISIONS

Christian suffering in the light of full salvation (1:1-2:8); the believer's life in view of his sevenfold position (2:9-4:19); Christian service in the light of Christ's coming (5:1-14).

4. OUTLINE

Introduction (1:1-12)
Conduct Before
God (1:13-2:10)
  Holiness, Love,
  Spiritual Growth,
  Praise
Conduct Before
Men (2:11-4:19)
  Submission to
  Authority

Submission to Persecution
Family Relations
Social Relations
Christian Example
Conduct of
Church (5:1-10)
Pastor, People
Conclusion(5:12-14)

5. SPECIAL CHARACTERISTICS

Peter is an important name in Scripture. While Paul's name is mentioned 162 times, and the rest of the apostles' names together are given 142 times, the name of Peter is mentioned 210 times.

Peter's letters bear close resemblance to Paul's. They open with a similar salutation, give thanksgiving and then conclude with that personal touch.

All the chief doctrines of Christianity are emphasized in Peter's writings; the suffering and death of Christ (2:24); the new birth (1:23); redemption by blood (1:18, 19); the Resurrection (3:20, 21); the return of Christ (1:7; 13; 5:4).

Peter is not mentioned in The Acts after chapter 15. But his visit to Syrian Antioch is given in Galatians 2:11. Also he must have labored chiefly among his own people (Gal. 2:8). Some think that his last years were spent in Rome where he is said to have suffered martyrdom. There is little evidence to substantiate this.

It is thought that Peter may have written this letter immediately after Paul's death and sent it by Silas (Sylvanus) to the churches which Paul had founded, to encourage them to bear up under suffering (5:12).

6. OUTSTANDING TEACHINGS

This book is the outstanding authority on the "why" of suffering. Peter reminds the flock that they were to share in the rejection and hatred of Christ (4:12-16). The coming of the Lord was to be their hope (4:7).

Wives were to be submissive, thus testifying of the grace of God. Servants were to be obedient even under oppression (2:18-20).

An illuminating commentary on inspiration is here given (1:10-12), where it is said that the Prophets studied carefully their own writings to learn God's truth.

Mark or Marcus (writer of second Gospel) was evidently with Peter (5:13) when this letter was written.

7. KEY TO UNDERSTANDING

In this book we are viewing some of God's eternal truth through Peter's pen. The broad outline is first suffering, then glory.

II Peter

1. BACKGROUND

Writer, the Apostle Peter (1:1); written possibly from Rome. If I Peter was written during Nero's persecution (A.D. 65) and if Peter was killed in this persecution, then this letter was written about A.D. 67

Occasion: Unlike most of the other epistles, there are no specific persons addressed. But because this is the "second epistle" (3:1) we may infer that it was written to the same people as the first. The need is to meet current dangers.

2. THEME

The churches in Asia Minor were being tried by severe persecution trials from without. To help them in this crisis Peter had written his first epistle. Now, they are threatened by heresies and apostacies, perils from within. To meet this danger, Peter writes the second letter. The purpose is to warn and exhort (3:17, 18). The key word is "knowledge" (1:2, 3, 5, 6, 8; 2:20, 21; 3:18).

3. MAIN DIVISIONS

The great Christian virtues (1:1-14); exaltation of the Scriptures (1:15-21); danger of apostate teachers (2:1-22); coming of Christ and Day of the Lord (3:1-18).

4. OUTLINE

Introduction (1:1, 2)
Preservation (1:3-21)
  Promises
  Progress
  Witness
  Word
Peril—False Teachers (2)
  Presence
Punishment
Perception
Perseverance (3)
  Mockery
  Mercy
  Wrath
  Watchfulness

5. SPECIAL CHARACTERISTICS

II Peter and II Timothy have much in common. Both foresee the coming apostacy. Paul sees the laity infected with this deadly virus; Peter warns of false teachers. Jude also views the same peril as he warns in all phases. But in none of these is to be found a note of pessimism or dejection. The promises of God are still wonderfully sufficient.

It is questioned if Peter was in Rome even at the time of Paul's death, as no mention is made of him in any of Paul's prison epistles. However, it could be possible that Peter arrived shortly following and that this letter was sent from there.

II Peter and Jude are much alike in certain passages. However, this is explained when we remember that the apostles often went on journeys together and listened to one another preach. Peter senses the nearness of his own death (1:15) and remembers that the Lord had foretold the manner (John 21:18, 19).

6. OUTSTANDING TEACHINGS

Seven divine qualities (1:5-11) are the fruits of the precious faith. They are steps from earth to heaven.

An important principle of Scripture understanding is given (1:20, 21) where we are told that no Truth is of private (by-itself) interpretation but that Scripture is to be compared and fitted together with other Scripture.

The attitude of the world toward the doctrine of the coming of Christ is given in the opening of chapter 3. In the same passage is taught the reason why Christ has not yet returned (3:9). The high esteem of Paul in Peter's mind is shown by his words "our beloved brother Paul" (3:15).

The tremendous subject of the end of the world and the culmination of time is graphically portrayed in the end of chapter 3.

7. KEY TO UNDERSTANDING

This Epistle could well be labeled with the words: "The

warnings against false teaching in the light of the sure accomplishment of God's purpose.

I John

1. BACKGROUND

Writer, John, the beloved Disciple, brother of James, son of Zebedee, a fisherman turned "fisher of men." Written from Ephesus.

John is also writer of the Gospel which bears his name, two other brief letters, and the closing book of the Bible, Revelation.

The date is late, about A.D. 95, near the close of John's eventful life, and some 60 years after the resurrection of Christ.

This letter, along with John's other writing, was composed some 30 years after the other New Testament books.

Occasion: John's Gospel had been written to show that Jesus Christ is the Son of God, and that by believing in Him, one might have life (John 20:30, 31). This letter, addressed evidently to Christians everywhere, emphasizes the assurance of those who already have been saved (5:13). Key words are "know" and "fellowship."

2. THEME

This is a family letter from the heavenly Father to His little children or His "born ones." The world is seen as without. God is here concerned about the behavior of His children. The moral government of the universe is not in question. Here the family is important. While the Gospel by John leads us across the threshold of the Father's house, the letters of John make us at home there. Paul, as he writes, is concerned about our public position as sons; John with our nearness to the Father. Next to the Song of Solomon, this is the most intimate of the writings of the Bible.

3. MAIN DIVISIONS

The family with the Father (1:1-3:24); the family and the world (4:1-5:21).

4. OUTLINE

Introduction (1:1-4)

Light (1:5-2:29)
  Perception
  Person and Purpose
  Perils
  Permanence

Love (3;4)
  Sons
  Seducers
  Brothers

Life (5)
  Witnesses
  Confidence

5. SPECIAL CHARACTERISTICS

This book is strongly characterized by the positiveness of the writer. John writes as one who had heard, seen, and handled the Son of God. The word "know" and kindred terms are used 40 times. There was great need in the church for this epistle. Heresies were creeping in which denied the verities of the faith. There were the Ebionites who taught that Christ was a mere man. The Cerinthians taught that Christ was an emanation of God that descended on the man Jesus and left Him before the cruicifixion. The Docetists held that Christ had no real body, and hence only appeared to suffer.

John was always a writer in love. But here he is very blunt as he unquestioningly and uncompromisingly points out false teachings and false teachers. He declares such is a spirit of antichrist.

According to tradition, John cared for Jesus' mother till her death. After the destruction of Jerusalem, John made his home in Ephesus. Among his "pupils" were such worthies as Polycarp, Papias, Ignatius.

6. OUTSTANDING TEACHINGS

Written to children, i.e., God's children, or Christians, only.

Prominent keys "Light," "Life," "Love."

Very important verse is 1:9 where Christians are told

what to do in case of sin.

Chapter 4 uses the word "love" more than any other in the Bible. God is declared (4:8) to be love, but the true manifestation of that love is shown in verse 9.

7. KEY TO UNDERSTANDING

Just remember that I John is from the Father to His children only.

II John

1. BACKGROUND

Writer, John, disciple, intimate friend of Christ, bishop of Ephesus, last remaining member of the Twelve; time, about A.D. 97, from Ephesus.

Occasion: This is one of John's personal letters. Along with III John, it is all we possess of the private correspondence of this disciple.

2. THEME

This letter is addressed to "the elect lady and her children" which may mean a woman of some prominence and influence whose identity had to be concealed for reasons not given.

She seems to be a woman of great hospitality, largely given to entertain missionaries in her home. Now knowing the dangers of false teachers, John writes to warn her against extending her generosity to those who were a menace to the Christian faith.

3. MAIN DIVISIONS

The pathway of truth and love (1-6); the peril of unscriptural ways (7-11); superscription (12. 13).

4. OUTLINE

Introduction (1-4)
  Salutation
  Thanksgiving
Commandment (5, 6)

Warning (7-9)
Exhortation (10, 11)
Conclusion (12, 13)

5. SPECIAL CHARACTERISTICS

The size of a letter in the Bible is actually no criterion of its importance.

The key phrase is "the truth" by which John means the body of revealed truth or the Scriptures.

The letter begins with John styling himself "the Elder." How appropriate, as John had outlived all the rest of the apostles and was now some 90 years of age.

6. OUTSTANDING TEACHINGS

We must remember that there is truth found in this small letter which is unique on all the pages of the Book of God. We must not miss it.

The "thy children" of verse 4 can either mean natural children, or possibly the members of the church in that city.

Large emphasis is given here against false teachers and deceivers as in I John. The criterion is again seen to be their testimony of Jesus Christ. (7).

In the American Revised Version verse 7 is rendered "who confess not that Jesus Christ **cometh** into the world." This suggests that the enemies denied both the first and the second coming of Christ.

The vital necessity of receiving Christ if one desires to come to God is taught in verse 9. To attempt to come to God another way is to be a thief and a robber (John 10:7-9).

Strict warning about receiving persons into one's home is given in verses 10, 11. The doctrine referred to here is the complete truth concerning the birth, life, death, resurrection, coming of Christ.

A delightfully intimate, friendly note is appended by verse 12.

7. KEY TO UNDERSTANDING

A "real" letter from dearly beloved John to a Christian mother.

III John

1. BACKGROUND

Writer, John, disciple, now bishop of Ephesus in Asia Minor; time is late, about A.D. 97, written from Ephesus.

Occasion: Evidently this letter is written to a wealthy man named Gaius (1:1) urging him to open his door for ambassadors of the true Gospel. The name Gaius is mentioned several times in The New Testament. (Acts 19:29; 20:4; Rom. 16:23; I Cor. 1:14), but we are uncertain if this is the same person.

2. THEME

There was a problem in one of the local churches. It seems that a certain man named Diotrephes was usurping power and rejecting apostolic authority and letters. John evidently had written to the church (9) and now writes to a certain man in the church in an endeavor to correct the disorder. Probably this is one of many such letters written by the apostles. This one, however, the Spirit of God has preserved for our instruction.

3. MAIN DIVISIONS

Personal greetings (1-4); instruction (5-8); two leaders contrasted (9-14).

4. OUTLINE

Introduction (1-4)	**Selfishness Condemned**
Salutation	(Diotrephes) (9, 10)
Thanksgiving	**Exhortation**
Hospitality Commended	(Demetrius) (11, 12)
(Gaius) (5-8)	**Conclusion** (13, 14)

5. SPECIAL CHARACTERISTICS

Together with II John they disclose the life and character of the members of the early church. Even as now, the believers had their imperfections. Pastoral oversight was necessary to adjust the difficulties.

Some think that Diotrephes was one of the false

teachers spoken of in I John. He had taken such power in his hands that he had refused to allow teachers or representatives who came from the Apostle John to minister in his church.

Paul had evangelized in this area some 40 years earlier. Later, John had come to be the leader of the community. Gathering round about him some preachers and teachers, he sent them into the surrounding countryside. Apparently in some areas, notably one in which Diotrephes lived, the evangelists of John had been refused. On their return, they told their story in John's home church (6). Now, they were going again to visit, taking with them this letter to Gaius.

6. OUTSTANDING TEACHINGS

The root trouble with Diotrephes was self-seeking, and rejection of apostolic authority. In this manner he becomes the dictator of the church, thus destroying the fellowship and communion with God's people everywhere.

Evidently there were good men too, in the church, among them Gaius who walked in the truth (3) and Demetrius who loved the truth and had a good report of all who knew him (12). These were exhorted to right the situation that existed.

That John purposed to come himself to the church is hinted in verse 14. Yet he hoped that the trouble would be past when he arrived.

In verse 2, John expresses a prayer that Gaius might prosper in "health" as well as in other things.

7. KEY TO UNDERSTANDING

A problem in one of the early Christian churches and God's answer for it.

Jude

1. BACKGROUND

Writer, Judo, half brother of the Lord (Mark 6:3), brother of James who wrote the Epistle of James, and a leader in the early church; time about A.D. 67.

Jude has much in common with II Timothy and II Peter, both deal with growing apostasy in the church.

Occasion: It seems that Jude had been planning to write a full and complete account of the "common salvation" (3) including his personal and intimate knowledge of the early life of the Lord. At this point he was restrained, and impressed to write concerning the growing apostasy.

The letter is a general one to the churches but probably had its first ministry in the churches addressed in Peter's epistles.

2. THEME

We are "to contend for the faith."

In the last part of the apostolic age there came many false teachers proselyting in the churches and drawing followers after them. The teaching of these "certain men crept in unawares" followed the line of idle speculation and philosophy and allowed their disciples to live in all manner of licentiousness. One of their corrupt doctrines was that God was too good to punish men on account of sinful indulgence. To expose such falsehoods Jude wrote this Epistle.

3. MAIN DIVISIONS

Introduction and occasion (1-4); apostasy is possible (5-7); such teachers described (8-19); comfort and assurance (20-25).

4. OUTLINE

Introduction (1-4)
National Apostasy (5-10)
 Illustration,
 Application

Individual Apostasy (11-16)
 Illustration, Application
Exhortation (17-23)
Conclusion (24, 25)

5. SPECIAL CHARACTERISTICS

Jude's letter is very similar to II Peter 2. Yet there is a difference as Peter speaks of apostasy coming, while Jude treats it as actually present.

The first result of the reading of the letter by Jude is the consciousness of the awfulness of sin. Perhaps this is the most forceful passage in the New Testament.

Jude mentions his relationship to James (1) possibly to give authority and weight to his letter. James was the honored leader of the church of Jerusalem, a distinguished and influential person.

Jude's knowledge of the unknown years of Jesus of Nazareth must have been full and wonderfully interesting. Yet, the Spirit of God must have forbidden such revelation, planning rather that the emphasis concerning Christ should be on His ministry, death and resurrection.

6. OUTSTANDING TEACHINGS

The frightful epithets Jude uses are not for vile people of the world, but for false teachers in the church.

The earliest prophecy of the second coming of Christ is given here and ascribed to Enoch (14, 15), who lived in 3800 B.C.

Insight into spiritual conflict is given in verse 9 where Michael, the archangel, is shown to be in conflict with the devil about the matter of the burial of Moses.

7. KEY TO UNDERSTANDING

A courageous, fighting letter against false teachers and a challenge to contend for the faith.

Revelation

1. BACKGROUND

Writer, John, disciple, bishop of Ephesus, now prisoner of Caesar and exiled to the island of Patmos off the coast of Asia Minor; time, about A.D. 96 from Patmos.

Occasion: Without a doubt John was allowed to be exiled to Patmos in order that God might give him this revelation which is the capstone of all Scripture. Later, John was released and took up his residence in Ephesus where he died.

2. THEME

The unveiling, the revealing, the disclosing of the true Person of Jesus Christ in all the wonder of His person and the glory of His work. This book is the grand climax to all the magnificent truths in the Bible's other parts. Without the Revelation, the Bible would be incomplete. Here we gather together all the threads of truth and weave them into one clear and complete picture.

3. MAIN DIVISIONS

The things which thou hast seen, the vision (1:19); the things which "are" (church age) (1:19); the things which shall be (coming events) (1:19).

4. OUTLINE

Introduction (1)
Seven Letters (2; 3)
Six Sevens (4-22)
    7 Seals

7 Personages
7 Dooms
7 Trumpets
7 Bowls
7 New Things

5. SPECIAL CHARACTERISTICS

Revelation abounds with Old Testament quotations. While Matthew contains 92 quotations, and Hebrews 102, Revelation has 285.

This is the one book of prophecy in the New Testament. Christ is seen to be the center and the circumference of all predictive writing. Everything that is to come is bound up in Him.

It should be noted that the subject is not plural, "revelations," but singular (1:1) "revelation," i.e., the revealing of the true person of the Son of God.

The writing of Revelation abounds in signs, symbols, mysteries. But we are to understand the truths of this book in a literal manner except when it is clearly symbolical or figurative.

Only once in the entire Bible is a special blessing promised to those who read and who hear (1:3).

6. OUTSTANDING TEACHINGS

The seven letters of chapters 2 and 3 have a fourfold application: (1) they were written to correct abuses in the actual churches named; (2) they apply to churches of all ages; (3) they have an individual application to all Christians of all ages; (4) they constitute an outline, historically, of the great church ages from the time of Christ to the coming of Christ.

The main section of Revelation is occupied with the great Tribulation period, including chapters 4-19. These chapters are further divided into 6 sevens (see Outline).

Revelation has a special relationship to Genesis. In that first book all things begin, including man, life, marriage, sin, etc. In Revelation we find the final disposition of man.

The most delightful truth of Revelation is found in the last chapters as heaven and its glories are thrillingly described. The final note however, is one of glorious invitation to come to Christ.

7. KEY TO UNDERSTANDING

Look for Christ in all of this book. Admittedly it is difficult, but the Spirit who wrote it will teach it to all who want to learn.

THOUGHTS AND INSIGHTS:

THOUGHTS AND INSIGHTS: